MW01200252

LIVED CHRISTIANITY

Dom François de Sales Pollien

CALX MARIAE
PUBLISHING

Original title: *Cristianesimo vissuto* (published by Marietti, 1958)

Translated into English by Brendan Young
from the 2017 edition © Edizioni Fiducia, Rome, Italy

Scripture quotations are from the Douay-Rheims version.

English edition © 2022 Voice of the Family, Calx Mariae Publishing
Calx Mariae Publishing is an imprint of Voice of the Family, London,
United Kingdom.

ISBN: 978-1-8384785-4-4

www.voiceofthefamily.com

CONTENTS

PART II: GOD ALONE

PART III: WORK

PART IV: THE EXERCISES OF PIETY

PREFACE

"Come, children, hearken to me: I will teach you the fear of the Lord. Who is the man that desireth life: who loveth to see good days?" (Ps 33:12-13); this is to say, I will teach you what it means to live. Do you know what it means?

Living does not mean wasting all of one's energy eating and drinking, or on what is attractive; nor does it mean dilating one's heart and distracting one's soul with exterior beauty. This is nothing other than what is popularly called "dragging out one's existence". To what end? To the slaughterhouse and to the sewer. It means one is wasting one's intelligence, profaning the heart, selling one's soul, selling one's very life by the hour. What is left of a life lived in this way? Emptiness and disgust, sterility and shame, remorse and punishment.

You are a Christian, you see life itself open before you, you feel it move within you. What an abundance of life-giving sap! Will you let it flow out uselessly? If only you knew what living treasures the One who created you has placed within you! O Christian heart so full of life, swear then not to waste anything, promise to use it until the last drop. If I could but convince you to take this oath, and to teach you to observe it: to swear to live, and then to keep this oath.

But here I address myself only to those men who hear and understand, to those who desire great things and have decided to live seriously and to the full. Those who want to be something for God, those who feel the pressing need to belong to Him completely, to give their life for God without hesitation, these are the only ones, to whom I make my appeal, because only they are capable of understanding me. If you are not one of them — close this book — my appeal is not for you.

There can be no half measures, no mediocre men, no half Christians: it is all or nothing. We deal in certainties, rigorous conclusions, cause and consequence, and we accept everything without batting an eyelid, proceeding with the coolness of reason and with the ardour of the Faith. No calculating interests! Vile pretexts and fearful distinctions are banned. Principles, absolute principles! Integral Christianity in the absolute fullness of its truth.

O heart, which God made so great, you are not made to drift along in half measures, to shuffle about the earth with your petty devices. Do you not feel the need for fresh air, full light, and substantial food? How can you reconcile yourself to living so shallowly and to die as a useless being? Come and learn the secrets of life in all its fullness and in its incomparable truth.

Let me say to you: be a man! Hear well: be a man; it is a great thing to be a man. And have integrity; you will never be a man if you do not have integrity. That is what I want to show you. Let me say to you: be a Christian. The Christian is the most perfect of the works of God. Be one, walking on your only path toward your only destination, without wandering either to the left or to the right. Are you resolved to be a Christian? To be one completely? To be one exclusively? Come, I will tell you what it means to be a Christian and how to become one.

But, I repeat, be bold and break with half measures and compromises; with mixing and matching teachings and compromising principles. If you continue to believe that you can "come to an arrangement" with Heaven, that the rights of God are not so pressing, that some words of the Gospel and of the Church can be chosen and others not; if you believe that the Faith is nothing but a cupboard in which certain ingredients are stored and occasionally used to appease the conscience, and that it should not enter into the particulars of everyday life; if you do not want to take the Faith in its truth and the Gospel in its bareness, if you are not willing to be a Christian in all places and situations, to be nothing other than a Christian, integral and absolute, without calculated interests, you will, in fact, not understand this book — put it down.

Here you will find ideas and ways of thinking diametrically opposed to those found in the world, in which principles are compromised in every possible way, trimmed, bent, and crumbled, according to the tastes of each person. But then one is seen to be unbending when it comes to certain conventions and pathetic little matters concerning one's own self-interest. Here principles are everything, and details count for very little; one is unbending when it comes to fundamental truths and extremely flexible in questions of means and practices. One becomes a servant of the truth whilst mastering trivialities; today, the world mutilates the truth as it sees fit, and becomes a slave of triviality. If you have the courage to look Christian life in the eye, and are fortunate enough to understand it in its true essence, you will see where to find true greatness and freedom of spirit; true life and happiness.

Believe me, in this book, there is more substance than one can digest in a first reading. Read it attentively and several times. I tell you that words hide more things than they express, sentences contain more than they suggest. I have written it to give you a key; if you pay attention to me, this key will open many horizons and many books to you — serious horizons and serious books — and equally, it will close off to you many false horizons and false books.

In our day, this has a very precious double advantage; but you will only truly appreciate it in the measure that you take advantage of the key I am placing in your hands. The better you learn to use it, the more you will realise the things it opens and closes. I hope that you will know how to use it to your advantage, and I ask you to pray a little for me, once you feel that I have done you some service.

PART I

GOD FIRST

I FAITH IN GOD

Do you believe in God? — "What a question!" you will say to me. — Yes, indeed, what a question! And what a great question! And I repeat it: *do you believe in God?* — "Yes," you tell me. — I answer: "Maybe." — "What do you mean, 'maybe'?"

Come now, believe me: there are two things about which you must be absolutely resolute: 1) never settle for mere words; and 2) never lie to yourself. You would not believe how much we live within the vanity of words, and in the lie of our own interests. If you are determined never to be satisfied with the surface meaning of a word without pene-trating the depths of the matter, and never to be flattered by any interest whatsoever; to absorb the truth in its fullness at any cost, despite feelings of revulsion and impracticability — then you can understand me.

So, do you believe in God? — "Yes, of course, and I love Him." — Do you believe that He exists? — "Yes, and I would give my life to affirm Him before unbelievers." — Do you believe that He created everything? — "Yes, and I adore His power, admire His wisdom, and bless His goodness." — Do you believe that it was He Who created you, too? — "Yes, and my greatest desire is to express my gratitude to Him." — But if He created you, why did He do it? —

"Oh! surely for Him and for Him alone. I know that being the Infinite One, above all, He cannot but act for Himself. He could never be a Worker employed by another." — Do you therefore believe that you were made completely for God? — "Yes, completely; He is my only goal, and He will also be my eternal rest. With great joy I address to Him the words of St Augustine: 'Thou hast made us for Thyself, O God, and our heart is restless until it finds its rest in Thee.'[1] I believe this, and I love what I believe and this is what I intend to live."

Good! you believe in God, so you have the seeds of the faith, and this is a great treasure. Now you have to come to grips with your faith. Having understood the premise, you need to draw the conclusions. It is necessary that you show your faith in works because you know that "faith without works is dead" (Jm 2:20). Along with the seed of faith you also receive the sincere desire to live by it. You feel the need and are firm in your resolution to be a Christian through and through: blessed be God! Now I want to bring your knowledge to the same level as your will. Because good will which is not enlightened runs the risk of going astray, and this misfortune is quite common.

You are made for God; that is, for His glory; you must glorify Him. This is the purpose of your life. The reason for your coming into this world, your time here below, your departure and your entry into eternity consist essentially of these words. Life is always in motion; it stirs, struggles and advances. To what destination? To the glory of God, and

---

[1.] St Augustine, *Confessions*, Book 1, Chapter 1.

if it does not reach that, it will end up in death. The deeds accomplished in life are innumerable, but its goal is one: and if so many deeds are not directed to that one goal then life becomes empty.

II THE GLORY OF GOD

You are made for God: if He gave you life then He gave it to you for His own sake. Therefore, the whole of your life must be directed toward Him and His glory. He could have not created you at all, but in creating you, He could not have given you another essential purpose. I use the word "essential", and you know what this word means in its philosophical sense. Essence is that which is of such necessity in beings and in their relationships that, without it, nothing could exist. The glory of God is in the essence of things: that is, glorifying Him is something so necessary to beings created by Him that, without it, no being would exist. It is not essential for you to exist, but from the moment you come into existence, it is essential that you exist for God.

"Fear God, and keep His commandments: for this is all man," says the Holy Ghost (Ecc 12:13). He does not say only that it is "all *of* man" but says, more energetically, "this is *all* man"; his whole purpose of being, all his dignity, all his greatness, all his life. Not even God could have assigned you another essential purpose. What a great happiness to glorify God in this world and in the next! The saints in Heaven are intent only on singing God's praises, and this must be your only occupation in the present life, since you are only in this transitory life in order to learn what you must do eternally. What a sublime destiny! I will guide you to know its greatness a little better.

III THE HAPPINESS OF MAN

God has created you for Himself, and He has created you also for yourself. — "How so?" — In that He wants you to be happy with Him. Happiness is also part of your destination. You feel how much you need happiness. Who put this need in you? He Who created you, pouring into all the parts of your being an insatiable thirst for happiness.

These are three manifestations of a love which God was absolutely not bound to give you. First of all, He created you freely; without being obliged. Then, He created you for happiness; even in creating you, He was not obliged to create you that way. Take a look and see if, like you, the beings below you, are made for eternal happiness. Thirdly, He created you for supernatural happiness; even in creating you for happiness, He was not obliged to call you to a happiness infinitely above your nature. Here, then, is the triple love of God Who created you out of love. He created you, and here is His first act of love; He created you for happiness, and here is His second act of love; He created you for an incomprehensible, infinite, supernatural happiness, and here is His third act of love. Has He loved you enough?

And you, will you be faithful to the principle from which you derive? Or will you belie your destiny? You are great in the ideas of God: will you be small in yours? God made you great, because He destined you for two great things: His glory (an infinite good) and your happiness (another infinite good). Will you, forgetful of your greatness, wish to sell your life to some base desire? Absolutely not. When someone has two infinites before him, how can he waste his time? You can glorify God without limits, you can be infinitely happy: your life can and must unfold into infinity; but will you be so half-hearted as to close yourself off in the least thing?

Happiness! Do you know what it is? God gave you faculties which have inclinations and needs. As long as the need is not satisfied by the presence of the object that responds to them, you feel something incomplete in yourself; you feel emptiness and pain, you are missing something; and this something causes you suffering. When on the contrary your faculties, making use of their natural inclinations, find the object suitable to them, they unite, and this object fills and satisfies them; and this fullness, specifically, is happiness.

Therefore, happiness is the rest that your faculties find in the object that satisfies and fills them. You are made to be filled and content, and your irrepressible need for happiness tells you this in a very obvious way. It is fullness that you need, the fullness of life. You will never be happy if you live only a half-Christian life. In how many indefinable ailments do countless souls languish, for the sole reason that they live in mediocrity, and God does not will that half measures should satisfy their aspirations! Fullness! The fullness of life! You are made for the fullness of the Christian life. But what then is the Christian life? Before asking yourself what the Christian life is, would it not be good to ask yourself first of all, what is life? This word has a meaning that should not be ignored.

IV LIFE

What is life? This is one of those embarrassing questions, which we are surprised to find ourselves unable to answer, despite the fact that we know very well what life is and it seems so clear. You know and feel that you have it, but you cannot say what it is exactly. I will try to tell you.

Life is the development of a vital principle. See the plant: a mysterious principle is contained in a small seed, created by the One Who is alive forever and ever and is the Author of life. This mysterious principle, which in turn, follows laws which are mysterious in their own right — dictated by God — goes on to cause the development of the plant, with its stem, branches, leaves, flowers and fruits. Development is, specifically, the life of the plant: development, which started from the seed and grew by virtue of this internal principle, according to its own laws. You see four things in the life of the plant: first of all, an internal vital principle, then a seed in which this principle is contained, then the laws that it follows and, finally, what it produces. The same thing happens in all life. In the life of an animal, as in that of a man, you find these four elements: the principle, the seed, the laws, the development. A living being is therefore an organism which, starting from a seed, develops according to its own laws by virtue of an internal vital principle.

You understand very well that the internal vital principle is the essential one of life. It is this which is contained in the seed, follows its own laws, and causes the development of life. Nothing is living, except that which develops regularly according to the laws of a vital principle. It is this principle that constitutes life because it causes the development of the living being. Thus, it can be said with truth that life is the development of a vital principle.

To produce life, the principle needs to follow its laws. Each life has its laws. Thus, you see that a lily does not resemble a rose, nor does a cat resemble a cockerel. Why? Because in each of these beings the vital principle has different laws of development. But you also see that a lily always resembles a lily, and a cat resembles a cat. Again, why? Because the vital principle has within it fixed laws; it does not depart from those laws, and if it does, it dies and there is no life. Therefore, the first necessity of life is respecting the laws of its development.

But there is another necessity. Ordinarily, the development of life is dependent on external conditions. Look at plants and animals: plants need a suitable climate and soil in order to develop, they often need attention and assiduous cultivation so that life can nourish itself in suitable conditions; animals have similar nutritional and environmental needs. If these conditions are lacking, life stops. It is therefore necessary to ensure the external elements, without which life cannot develop. This is the second condition for life to exist.

I ask you to not be afraid of these philosophical principles; if necessary, have them explained to you. I want your faith to be solid, and to be solid, it must have foundations, and it cannot be founded except on principles.

V THE SCIENCE OF LIFE

To protect and preserve life (which is of the utmost importance), and to provide it with a favourable environment (which is of almost equal importance), one must have knowledge of it. How is it possible to care for what is unknown?

Look at the gardener: how hard he works to obtain beautiful results! He studies the theory and observes his plants — the laws they follow in their growth, the soil they need, the care they demand. In this way, he acquires the knowledge required of a gardener. Once in possession of this knowledge, he is able to protect and nurture the life of his plants. But what can he do who has no knowledge? He will ruin everything. Try to grow a plant which you do not understand, and you will see that your first task is to learn, observe, and try; at the risk of ruining your plant. So, to grow a plant, you need knowledge. In other words: knowledge of life is necessary to life. The science of life is the knowledge of the laws of development and of environmental needs: knowing how it develops and what environment it requires; knowing how it develops, in order to protect its growth from error, injury, deviation, pressure: all things which, by obstructing life, end up killing it; knowing what environment it requires, in order to provide it with beneficial elements and nutrients, and to protect it from being poisoned.

Every life requires the study of such science: the life of the plant you wish to cultivate, that of the animal you want to raise, your own life that you must develop. To live, one must know how to live. You who have the noble ambition of wanting to live in a Christian way; you who are resolved at all costs to develop the most incomparable of lives in yourself; do you understand the need, in which you find yourself, of knowing beforehand what Christian life is? Do you understand that your most urgent need is to have the knowledge of Christian life?

What a great science is that of Christian life! All science is beautiful; but that of life surpasses everything. And since Christian life surpasses every other life, the science of the Christian life is the greatest of the sciences. What value is there in all the others, if you do not have this one? And what can be lacking to him who possesses it? Knowing how to live in a Christian way: this is the science, the fundamentals of which I now want to teach you. Therefore, let us study together the conditions of your life, in order to form, according to your wishes, an entirely and truly Christian life.

VI THE LIFE OF THE BODY

God gave you life for His glory and for your happiness. And what life did He give you? First of all, He gave you the life of the body: natural life, by which the body lives through the soul and the soul lives in the body.

You know the principle and the operations of this life: the principle is the soul, given that the union of the soul and the body is what causes the body to be alive; the operations are knowledge, love and action. Thus, you have cognitive powers, will power, and operational powers: a set of powers for knowledge, which are the five senses, the imagination and the mind; a set of powers to love and to will (insofar as loving and willing are the same thing, since to love is to will the good) — one can say that this set of powers resides in external feelings, in sensitivity and in the will; a set of powers to act, ranging throughout all the limbs of the body.

"Man," says de Bonald, "is mind, heart and senses".[2] Here, the mind indicates all the cognitive faculties, because it dominates and directs them. The heart includes all the faculties of the will. We have made it clear not to take words too lightly; "heart" is a word that the ignorance of our day abuses terribly, assigning to it nothing more than passion and emotion. Remember that in Christian language the heart and the will are synonymous, and that they indicate all the faculties of the will. Finally, the senses indicate the power of the will. So, when God says, "thou shalt love the Lord thy God, with thy whole mind", He means *with all your will power*; and "with thy whole soul, and with thy whole strength" means *with all your operational faculties* (Mk 12:30).

Knowing, loving and acting: this is the complete activity of man; to develop the mind, heart and senses is your whole life. Do you want to live? Develop your mind, develop your

---

[2] Louis Gabriel Ambroise, Viscount de Bonald, *Théorie du pouvoir politique et religieux dans la société civile, démontrée par le raisonnement et par l'histoire* (*Theory of Religious and Political Power in Civil Society, Demonstrated by Reason and by History*), Book III, *On Education*.

heart, develop your senses, and you will live. Form for yourself a right mind, an energetic heart, and robust senses; that is, health of the mind, health of the heart, health of the body; and do not neglect anything, do not fake anything, do not break anything; in this way, you will live.

God made you to live; and to live is to develop. You do not know the extent of the resources of intelligence, dedication and action that God has placed in you. When a man knows how to focus all his strength, without letting go of any, he has an exceptional power. The most powerful man is not the one who has the greatest talents, but the one who wastes least. So, this is one kind of life that you possess: the life of the body, the natural life. It certainly has its greatness, its faculties: intelligence, will and action, which place man above all other visible beings. A person's life is the highest of all those that exist on the earth. Human life is indeed a great thing, and knowing how to develop it is a great science. Reflect on this! Instruction, education, formation: these are required to develop the mind, heart and senses of man, and they present no small problem!

VII THE LIFE OF THE SOUL

For most men, this natural life, which is made up of knowledge, love and action, is the whole of life. For you, who wish to be a Christian, this is only a small part, it is like the preparation for real life. The true life of the Christian is supernatural.

What is this supernatural life? It is that by which God gives life to the soul, just as the soul gives life to the body. All the operations of intelligence, love and action are performed by the soul in the body, and through it. In your Christian soul, God carries out the same operations of intelligence, love and action; that is to say, He takes possession of your natural faculties, and makes them act supernaturally. Natural life, rather than supernatural life, carries out the functions of the body. Natural life is the union of the soul with the body; supernatural life is the union of the soul with God.

This is most likely very mysterious to you, and you might not have a clear understanding of it yet. But it is precisely that which you are being taught about here, and later you will see it clearly. Just remember this: that you must be united to God, as the body is united to the soul; that God must give life to the soul, as the soul gives life to the body; that God must move the soul, as the soul moves the body. If it is such a great dignity for a human body to be united with a rational soul, how much greater the dignity for a Christian soul to be united to its God! If the education of the mind, the instruction of the heart and the formation of the senses of man in his natural life are such formidable problems, how great is the science which accustoms the mind, heart and senses to being moved by God and for God! You will see to what magnificent developments such a life is destined. You will see how great is the life to which you aspire.

How much you must thank God for having placed this wonderful and overwhelming need in the inmost part of your being, which makes you aspire to the depth and fullness of this life! Become a Christian, expand your spirit, heart and senses in the infinite surroundings of the supernatural life. How sweet, sublime and intoxicating! The man who enters into this real life feels that his whole being is made to climb to that point. As long as your soul is not fully free to expand itself to the supreme heights of the Christian life, you will feel that you are missing something. But when you realise that you are walking the path of life without obstacles, you will understand that you lack nothing — except Heaven, which is its crown.

The soul, animated by the divine movement of supernatural life, becomes capable of giving infinite glory to God, and of enjoying infinite happiness. If you were not a Christian, if you did not have the divine life within you, you would have only a very limited and incomplete natural capacity to praise God and to feel joy. But by virtue of divine union, you will acquire an infinite power of praise and joy. God, Who prepared and adapted your nature to this supernatural state, makes you feel, by the emptiness of earthly things, that you are made for infinity. If you only knew the greatness of your soul!

VIII THE LIFE OF THE CHURCH

The greatness of your soul! If you want to understand it, do not content yourself to develop your life in isolation. God did not create you to live isolated in this world, and He has not destined you to live alone in Heaven. Down here, as up there, He has predestined you to live in the unity of a great body, of which you must be a member, and that is the

Church of the saints. All angels and all men, by their very creation, are called to glorify God and to be beatified; to live united together, for this glory and for this happiness, in the organic, living, eternal unity of the Church.

"For many are called, but [alas] few chosen" (Mt 20:16). There are wicked angels and bad men who, because of sin, will not enter the Body of God's elect. You who are already part of this Body through Baptism and through the Christian Faith, who are resolved to "labour the more, that by good works you may make sure your calling and election" (2 Pt 1:10); consider its greatness, so as not to lose its benefit. "Giving thanks to God the Father, who hath made us worthy to be partakers of the lot of the saints in light: who hath delivered us from the power of darkness, and hath translated us into the kingdom of the Son of his love, in whom we have redemption through his blood, the remission of sins ... And he is the head of the body, the church, who is the beginning, the firstborn from the dead; that in all things he may hold the primacy" (Col 1:12–14,18).

You know that Jesus Christ is the Son of God made man. He is God and man. In Him God and man are so united that they form but one Person. Divine union is so complete in Him, so incomprehensible! It is the mystery of the Incarnation. It is through Him that God is truly and infinitely glorified; and it is through Him that angels and men are united to God. He is the Head and we are the members. All of the elect, both angels and men, each enter as a member, a living element in the great Body, of which Jesus Christ is the Head. Each one has his place marked, and his determined function; you and I are called to our own place and our own function.

Do you know why God gave you this mind, this heart, this body? Why each of us has an existence of a particular length, a certain number of faculties, various tendencies? Why gifts and graces vary for each individual? This happens also with the different elements of your body: the nerves, the veins, the bones, the fibres; each part has its own physiognomy, its structure, and its place according to its function. We are like this in the Body of Christ.

Why did God create angels so numerous and with such qualities? Why did He create — and why does He continue to create — men if not to answer the needs of the great Body of the elect. He outlined the plan, He knows to what extent it must develop, and the history of humanity here below will not end until the moment when the last member has brought about its fullness. What then is taking place as the history of the world unfolds? What is the result of the universal activity of beings? It is the formation of the great Body, in which, all together, the elect in Jesus Christ, praise God and enjoy Him.

What are you doing in this world? You grow, develop and come to occupy the place that God has assigned you, in order to fulfil as well as possible your eternal function for His glory and for your happiness. Tell me, would you still dare to waste your life, to condemn yourself to an eternal diminishing in which you would be only a half or a quarter of yourself; in which you would give God only a part of the praise due to Him, and would have for yourself but a part of the happiness that you were capable of in God's plans?

Think about it, an eternal decrease; to remain a disabled member in this Body of saints, for which God made you, to which you are already united! Oh, I implore you, do not insult Jesus Christ your Head, the Church, the saints and yourself: be a Christian worthy of your name, worthy of your vocation, worthy of your God. If only you had faith — faith in God, faith in your immortal destiny — if only you could believe so much as never to lose sight of your divine greatness!

IX THE TOOLS OF LIFE

Now you know what your purpose is: to glorify God and make yourself happy. You know what you are: mind, heart and senses. You know what your natural life consists of: developing your body, your heart, your mind. You know what your supernatural life consists of: fulfilling yourself in God and in the Church. Thus, you know the purpose and make-up of your life; what more do you still need to know? The tools of life.

One does not send a gardener to work without tools, nor a soldier into to battle without weapons. However well one knows the job, and however strong one is, nothing can be done without tools. God created you, gave you a great task to perform and powerful strength to perform it. Has He not also given you the tools related to your task and to your strengths? Oh, bless Him, for here you will again admire His love. Yes, He gave you tools without number and without measure; you have an infinite assortment; you will never lack tools, and you will never use them all.

Now, do not complain that God has been stingy with you. You know that He has not restricted you in the horizon of your work, because it is infinite. You do not know what exceptional strength He has given you, because you are too used to wasting it. But, even more, you ignore the rich collection of tools He puts in your hands. An infinite work, incalculable strength, tools without number; this is what He has given you. Will it be His fault if you do not know how to expand your life? — "But, what are these tools?" — All creatures. Understand this well: all creatures. This word and its meaning must be clearly remembered.

"But what do you mean by creatures?" — By this word, it is necessary to understand that we mean all that is created, everything that is between God and you, all that God has made, and everything that He continues to make. What creatures are between God and you? Material creatures, such as the elements, water, air, fire, food, plants, animals and men, and all the events that take place; and spiritual creatures: grace, the virtues, the sacraments, the Church, the gifts of God, etc. How many things there are, and things which happen! All these things which exist and take place, are but tools for you. And you think you lack them?

Do you know what is meant by tools? It means here that everything which is and everything which happens is destined by God to serve you in the great work of your life. He places everything at your disposal; nothing exists, and nothing happens except for you to use as a tool. This is the counsel of God: this is the reason for all created beings and for all the movements of those beings, human and divine. "And we know," says St Paul "that to them that love God, all things work together unto good, to such as, according to His purpose, are called to be saints" (Rom 8:28).

X THE COUNSELS OF GOD

Do you now understand the counsels that God has for you and all beings created by Him? Is it not magnificent? He has an essential purpose: His glory. To this essential purpose, He adds a second: the happiness of His elect. To achieve this, He has a master plan: the union of all His elect with Him, and among themselves, through Jesus Christ. To carry out this plan, He subsequently created angels and men; each destined to take his place and to fulfil his role in the great Body of Christ.

Giving each member the honour of being formed by Him personally, He gives life at the stage of a seed, which He must cultivate until full growth. And to work towards this growth, He creates tools without number: the creatures which He Himself uses and which you too must use. This is the general economy of creation and the existence of all things, and here is the organisation of the special plan of your life in the counsel of God. Meditate profoundly on His counsel and it will explain everything to you: you will understand God, yourself, and the world. You will understand your life, and you will also understand your lethargy and weakness up until now.

No doubt, at first glance, you will not see how all these tools can be useful: you are so unfamiliar with using them, and you know so little of their usefulness! But you will learn, and life for you will have incomparable splendours; and you will be happy to feel your life expand for God without measure.

God is what He is; you are what God made you, and things are what God made them. He is the Infinite One. He made you for Him, and things for you. Are you presuming, perhaps, to recast this plan of God? Instead, recast your ideas according to this plan, and you will see that there is a lot to be done. If you know so little about living, the reason is that you stray too far from the counsel of God; you will see this more clearly later.

O Christian heart, how fortunate you are to have faith! You still have time to correct your ways, to direct your life towards its proper end. By no means are the resources of life in you used up, and you will know how to use them. May they bless God!

XI THE END OF CREATURES

Creatures are tools, but tools of what? Essentially of the glory of God, and secondly of your happiness. They must serve you in gaining these two goods, which are the sole purpose of your life. They therefore have a double usefulness: the first — essential and primary — for God; the other — ancillary and secondary — for you: divine usefulness and human usefulness.

As tools, they have a wonderful aptitude for serving these two purposes: in fact, they are the work of God; and you must believe that, when God prepares tools, they are divinely suited to the work for which they are intended. If man knows how to manufacture tools so skilfully for his work, will God be less able than he? You would never dare to insult Him by believing that He has not known how to adapt His works to His counsels. The saints, who are no strangers to the counsels of God, know that creatures are precise instruments for those who know how to live.

In the hands of an ignorant man, familiar with neither the work nor the tools, even the best tool is worth nothing. Give the tool to a tradesman and then you will see. Who are the tradesmen for the job we are talking about? They are the saints. What powerful and effective tools creatures are in their hands! What works the saints have accomplished with the very tools that you do not know how to handle! If only you knew how to ask these masters the secrets of your work in this world. Here I want to teach you some of them and I hope you will be able to take advantage of them.

XII THE USE OF CREATURES

Creatures are tools. How should you make use of them? First of all, you have to use them, and not serve them. You must have them in your hand and not in your heart, says St Augustine.[3] And this short sentence says a lot. They are tools, nothing else. None of them is your purpose, God alone is

---

[3.] St Augustine, *Sermons*, 177, No. 3.

your purpose; apart from Him there is no trace of purpose for your faculties; everything is a means, everything is a tool. Neither your mind, nor your heart, nor your senses have any purpose in creatures; they find tools there, and that is all.

And how do you use a tool? In the work for which it was made, and in the measure — no more and no less — that it is useful. You take a pen for writing, a knife for cutting, a needle for sewing. You pick them up when needed, you use them for as long as you need to, and afterwards you put them back. That is a tool, and how to use it. That is how you should act with everything. To use things in this way, you need to know their usefulness. The child does not know how to use anything, because he does not know the usefulness of anything. He will put a knife in his mouth as much as he will a piece of bread, he will play with fire as he will with a picture. You already know a lot about the human usefulness of creatures; but what do you know of their divine usefulness? Seek your happiness there, and I will tell you how, later on. But the glory of God! You do not even suspect your ignorance in this regard.

Pay close attention to these principles, which are full of conclusions that will develop later, and from which you will not be able to escape. You know, we made a pact never to lie to ourselves, and to always get to the bottom of things. Believe me, the bottom of this word "tools" is strangely deep; so try to fathom it, and make sure that you don't get dizzy.

One must be a man: with a positive mind, an energetic heart, and a strong body.

XIII ORDER

Who is going to come first, you or God? — "What a question!" — It seems strange to you, doesn't it? — "Of course, so why ask me? Is this a question to ask ourselves?" — A little while ago, I asked if you believed in God, and that first question surprised you as much as this one; remember both of them. I warn you now that I will remind you of them, and then your surprise will be even greater.

For the moment it seems evident to you that, if God is God, He must be first in everything. His glory therefore always comes before your happiness: this is the order of purpose. Your faculties must then be concerned with His glory more than with your happiness: that is the proper order of your work. Therefore, creatures too must serve His glory rather than your happiness: this is the proper order of tools. Isn't all this as clear as daylight?

It is the essential right of God to be first in everything. "Lord, who is like to thee?" (Ps 34:10). If it is His right then it must be respected. Would you dare not respect the rights of God? And if you did not respect them, would He not make you respect them sooner or later? Order is order, and, says St Augustine, "the blessedness of order is such that it can never be violated without vindicating itself."[4]

So I repeat: the essential order of things requires that the glory of God be set above your happiness, as much as God is above you. The essential order of your faculties is that your spirit, heart and senses occupy themselves with the

[4.] St Augustine, *De libero arbitrio (On the Free Choice of the Will)*, III, No. 44.

glory of God in the first place, and with your happiness only in the second place. The essential order of tools requires that creatures be used first of all for the glory of God, and in the second place towards your happiness. As long as God is God, and man is man, this will be the order of things. To presume to arrange things differently would be to deny God and deny man.

XIV DISORDER

Do you know how many evils there are in the world? There is only one; all evils derive from one alone. What is this evil, the father of all evils? It is the overthrow of the divine order; man puts himself in God's place, puts his pleasure before the glory of his Creator, and lives for himself rather than for God. This is disorder.

In the mind, the heart and the senses, human pleasure takes precedence; it takes first place everywhere, acquires a prevalent importance in life. The glory of God is relegated to second place, sometimes forgotten and sacrificed. Man no longer reserves for God the essential place that belongs to Him: God is no longer first, neither in the mind, the heart, nor in the senses of man. And creatures that must be used above all for God, are instead used almost exclusively for the pleasure of man. Instead of knowing, loving and serving God, man is concerned with knowing, loving and serving his own pleasure.

You see, in the earthly paradise the first woman and the first man perpetrated that great disorder, which was the starting point of all others. And what did they do? They preferred their pleasure to the divine order. And all other evils are derived from this first one. Son of Adam, you are born in original sin, and you carry a congenital disorder imprinted in your nature, which entices you to prefer your own satisfaction to the glory of your Creator. And human passions stir in everyone; and in everyone they tend to the same disorder. The search for oneself and one's own pleasure, to the detriment of God, is everywhere. Everywhere the creature is misused by man to the benefit of his sensualist egoism. The struggle of human pleasure against the divine order is everywhere.

Therefore, all creation is made false. Man is made false, because he is not in his place, and does not tend to his purpose; his faculties are distorted, because they do not act directly; creatures are made false, because they are ill used: God's plan is made false because it is overturned. What a mess!

And how can we be surprised if this disorder carries with it so many evils and so much ruin? St Paul says that "every creature groaneth and travaileth in pain" so as to free itself from this evil (Rom 8:22). You do not perceive this universal groaning; and, even though you feel that there is a lot of evil around you, you do not feel that there is much suffering in you!

XV MORTAL SIN

You commit evil sometimes; and what is the evil you commit? The most terrible evil, the greatest disorder, is mortal sin. And what is mortal sin? It is a created pleasure, to which you join yourself, and which you take up in a way that is so contrary to God's order and plan, that you overturn and destroy His glory by trampling on it and breaking the union of your soul with Him.

Mortal sin is a pleasure: in fact, you never offend God unless it is to obtain a pleasure that matters more to you than He does. It is a pleasure either of the mind, the heart or the senses. See, for example, the satisfaction of pride in your thoughts, the enjoyment of disordered affection in your heart, the seductions of guilty acts in your senses. Examine the encounters in which your poor soul lets itself slip into the abyss of evil. The pleasure which dominates you and drags you down is everywhere and always. Whether you commit mortal sin to obtain a pleasure that you seek, or to avoid an inconvenience you fear, you always follow the path of satisfaction.

And where does this path lead you? To injure your Creator and kill your soul: a grave, vulgar, incomprehensible injury to your Creator; this is the most deplorable part of your sin.

You do God the bloody injury of trampling underfoot His Name, His love, the fear of Him — in a word, His glory — to satisfy yourself with a pleasure that He condemns. Trampling God under your feet! As if God was meant to be under your feet? Do you believe in Him? Who comes first, you or Him?

And what a disaster in your soul! Offending God, you break with Him, you separate your soul from Him; you destroy within yourself that divine union which is your supernatural life. Your soul loses that supernatural activity, which is your true life as a Christian. This is the death blow to that which is best and highest in you, your existence as a Christian; whence derives the terrible epithet of "mortal". Tell me, where do you stand in terms of fear of this abomination? Do you feel its monstrosity? Are you determined, at any cost, forever to purge your mind, heart and senses of it? If only you had faith! If only you believed in God! If only you believed in the supernatural life! If only you knew the dignity of your Christian soul and the greatness of your life! No, it is impossible to have faith, true and living faith, sincere and profound faith, and not detest mortal sin above all other misfortunes.

As long as you hate this evil by halves, and reluctantly; as long as your heart voluntarily retains some sympathy for it, do not tell me that you are a man of faith. Sin has undoubtedly planted numerous deep roots in your soul, which are not in your power to eradicate in a day. But if you cry out over your evil, if you ask God to be freed from it, if you try to eradicate it, if you are generous in getting back up again, generous in fighting, this is enough for your faith. What God asks, what faith demands, is that you not remain voluntarily turned towards evil; that you be sincere and that, in the innermost part of yourself, you resolve simply to give

God His place. After that, if your weaknesses cause you a few more falls, God will heal them.

Therefore, I implore you to have faith, to believe in God; it suffices never to prefer a mortal pleasure to Him; put this first, at the top of your consciousness, once and for all. Resolve to die rather than voluntarily to let the obscene monster profane you, trample the glory of God, defile your soul and kill your life. Yes, the death of the body a thousand times, rather than that of the soul.

XVI VENIAL SIN

Here is an incomparably less serious evil than the preceding one, given that it does not have such dire consequences, either before God or for yourself. Nevertheless, it is still the same movement of your soul towards created pleasure. What is venial sin, in fact? It is created pleasure towards which you are attracted, to which you join yourself, and which you take up, contrary to the order and plan established by God, in such a way as to damage His glory and your soul. It is pleasure, since this is the only thing that attracts and deceives your soul, so as to distract it from God; it is pleasure either of the mind, heart, or senses. It is a satisfaction, whose charm dominates you, and from which you do not know how — or do not want — to free yourself.

You remain attached to it, and are enticed by it. Enticed where? To the point of wounding God and your soul. You wound God's glory. It does not destroy His glory in you, but it maims, falsifies, affects and violates it, more or less, according to the number and importance of your sins. Tell me, is God perhaps meant to be a laughing stock for you? Does He deserve so much contempt on your part? Do you believe in Him? Who must be first, Him or you?

You wound your soul. Venial sin in itself does not go so far as to bring on death; but how many bruises, wounds, and how much maiming! Do you think that God has given you your soul so that you can mistreat it in such a strange way? Is the supernatural life, then, so despicable to you, that it is necessary to treat it so unworthily? You are careful not to cause wounds to your body, and when, in spite of yourself, a misfortune comes to damage your health, how much care you expend to repair and heal it! Is your body therefore more precious than the soul? Do you thus expect me to recognise in you a man of faith? When one truly believes in God, one does not hurt Him with a cheerful heart. When one believes in the supernatural life, one takes the greatest care not to harm it, or to repair it if it is hurt. God and the soul are the two sacred things which faith teaches you to respect, to love, and to honour above all else.

Where do you stand in regard to venial sin? Do you not gulp it down like water? Do you not swallow it like air? So many thoughts, affections, actions! Pride, with all its base-ness, ambitions, jealousy, its lack of charity; and sensuality, with all its insanity, its quests, its cowardice, its gluttony, its lust, its amusements, and the whole incalculable parade of faults that the search for pleasure drags along with it and puts before the glory of God. Note that I presume you only glance at all these shortcomings of pride and sensuality, and they do not lead you to serious sins. But even if they are light, how much more numerous they are! Is it not perhaps true that your mind is full of venial thoughts? And what about the affections of your heart? What about your actions? How many flaws are in all of this! And you almost don't care! You say: "But this is not a mortal sin." And you believe in God? You believe that God is God, and yet you trample Him underfoot like this, and torment Him with so many blows? You will tell me that you love your father very much, because the only thing you do is beat him every day, but you have not killed him yet?

Believe in God, once and for all, and give Him first place. When you have cast out the devil of venial sin from all the thoughts of your mind, from all the affections of your heart, from all the actions of your senses; when no habit of venial pleasure reduces the glory of God in you; when you are willing to die, rather than to deliberately consent to trampling God underfoot with the slightest venial offence: then I will start to believe that you are beginning to know what God is, and to have that firm faith in Him that befits His greatness and the dignity of your soul.

Undoubtedly, human weakness must be taken into account — and very much into account. We will fall many more times, we will still offend the One Whom we must love and Whom we wish to love; we will still offend His love. "For a just man shall fall seven times," says the Holy Ghost; but, the sacred text immediately adds, and "shall rise again" (Proverbs 24:16). So, you will still be surprised, despite your good desires and your good will. If you are truly just, you will get back up. By this is the just man recognised. You must not be surprised, frightened or discouraged by your weakness; God will heal it. Be sincere and upright; you will see later how He heals and leads upright souls.

XVII   THE EVIL THAT YOU DO NOT KNOW

Will you be in good standing with God once you have cast out all consent to venial sin, even to the last trace? Will He then have the place in your life which befits Him? Will He be the first in everything, once and for all? You will no longer offend Him at all voluntarily. What a great thing! And how ardently you yearn for it! How you long to finally put your life in order, in accordance with your faith! How you swear not to lie to yourself any longer! — "God is God, and He will be my God, and I will treat Him as God." This is your oath, is it not? Yes, you are indeed determined this time to believe in God and put Him first.

No more sins! Sin is an abominable lie in a man who has faith. It is unworthy of a self-respecting man constantly to belie his beliefs. Honour requires all or nothing. Either I do not believe in anything, or I go all the way with my duty. Very good! No more sins. But are you definitively in full agreement with your faith? — "And how would I not be so?" you ask me. — Let's see. Does life consist only in avoiding evil? — "No, we must also do good." — Yes, and, thanks be to God, despite the abundance of shortcomings which still devastate your soul, I believe that actions good in themselves are more numerous in your life than bad ones.

In fact, occasions of sin do not infallibly present themselves at every moment: they are fairly frequent, but subject to interruptions.

Your life, on the other hand, does not undergo any interruptions. Your mind, your heart and your senses are in perpetual activity. All this activity is good in itself, and its operations, occurring one after the other uninterruptedly, are far more numerous than those of sin. There is a lot of good in you: it is in your thoughts, in your affections and in your actions. But how do you do this good? Who is your first priority, you or God? You know that, if you believe in God, you cannot concede that He should move to second place and you to first, in anything. Whenever you do good, or believe yourself to be doing good, I would like to know what place God's interest has, and what place your interest has. I am afraid that you behave like a rude person who serves himself first, goes first, speaks about himself first, and does not know how to be courteous to a fellow diner or visitor.

Do you observe the rules of etiquette towards God that you would not dare omit with a man? You know how to give way very elegantly, to yield first place, to offer refreshment, to name another ahead of you as etiquette dictates. But do you know, to the same extent, the standards that you must observe regarding God?

If in the good you do, or think you do, you put God in second place, you commit an evil, which is not a sin but an imperfection. This is what a lack of etiquette regarding God is called. You commit this incivility, because you do not know how to inconvenience yourself for Him; as you are used to looking out for your own comfort; since you think about your pleasure more than about Him. Once again, pleasure is the cause of your shortcomings in this regard, which are far more numerous than you might think. Your imperfections! Do you want me to tell you some of them? Do you want me to question your thoughts, your affections and your actions?

XVIII   WHERE DO YOU STAND?

We have understood that, if you have faith in God, you must put Him first: in your thoughts, your affections, your actions; in your whole life. It this not so?

First of all, in your thoughts. To know your thoughts, I listen to your words. I hear you talking about everything: people, things, events. You know how to appraise and judge; but from what point of view, from yours or God's? You measure all things by their usefulness; this is how it must be, since all things are nothing but tools, and a tool has no value other than its usefulness. But what usefulness do you acknowledge? Your own, no doubt. You know how much pleasure, interest, honour, and so on, people, things and events mean to you. You acknowledge human usefulness in all its aspects well enough. You know what is good or bad for you, that is, what you like and what you dislike; since it is through this lens that you see everything.

You say: this is lovely weather, bad food, good company, a disgraceful event, a splendid party, a decent job ... Whose interest comes into play here if not your own? This is the interest of man. Yes, what you see in all things is your own interest; it dominates all your ideas. Find one thing that you say in your assessments of the practical things of life — good or bad — which does not relate to yourself or to others. Where is God's interest? What place does it hold in your ideas? Creatures are tools — of what? Of the glory of God first of all; such is their essential usefulness. You take no notice of this. Your ideas are therefore false in everything.

When will you have the right idea? When will you be able to put God at the forefront of your thoughts? How long will it take to get used to relating your interest to God's, and to ordering and subordinating the development of your life, effectively and regularly, to His glory? You think of yourself, and of everything else for yourself; will you ever think of Him, and of yourself and all other things for Him? Even supernatural things, how do you judge them? You go about saying: what a great sermon, what a beautiful ceremony, what a good communion! Why? Because you have experienced a great satisfaction in your feelings. Your pleasure even informs you of the value of your communions.

In religion, that which is of the highest order is your salvation. Your salvation — your supreme happiness — is still you in this context: it is still your interest. In religion, you see a means of salvation, and this is perhaps the highest concept of religion that you have. But you do not go so far as to think that God has rights for Himself because He is God, and for the sole reason that He is God. If your salvation were not concerned, would you think a lot about God? The apex of your religion therefore consists in seeing yourself first. Your ideas about religion are therefore also completely wrong. Do you believe in God? Who must be first, Him or you?

"But, do I really not need to think any more about my salvation?" — Certainly, you have to think about it and you cannot think about it enough. But why let it come before the glory of God? This is not the right order. — "But if I save myself, I glorify God." — For my part, I think the opposite is true: if you glorify God, you will obtain salvation in return. You must not separate His glory from your salvation but put it before it; because God must be first and you second, since His rights come before your hopes, because He is God and you are man. Are you beginning to understand that it is a great thing to believe in God?

Know, then, that religion consists more in respecting the rights of God than in saving your hopes; more in glorifying God than in blessing yourself. The essential thing in religion is the honour of God; the ancillary thing is the happiness of man, which necessarily follows the honour of God. It follows and does not come before it. Get hold of the right ideas. If, in religion, we continue to see only a question of salvation — that is, of human usefulness — then we have come to what is commonly thought today; namely that, as long as human interests have not been harmed, we have accomplished our duty — our entire duty. The rights of God are no longer considered. When will you consider them?

XIX WHERE DO YOU STAND? (CONTINUED)

What about your loved ones? Do you know how many things you love? If you cannot count them, I will give you the exact number: you love only one thing, and that is yourself.

Let us take the rule outlined by St Augustine, which you will understand immediately. "A thing that is not loved for itself, is not loved."[5] Does that seem obvious to you? You love food, for example: but why do you love it? For the usefulness and for the pleasure you find in it. It is therefore not the food that you love, but yourself in it. Plumb the depths of all the things you love, all of them, and see if you do not attach yourself solely to what you like, hating what you dislike.

The rule of your affections is your interest in pleasing yourself. That is to say, you love for your own sake and are not capable of loving otherwise. Do you love God Himself in any other way than this? You love Him for the good He does you, or for what you expect of Him. If you loved His gifts for His own sake, and for the sake of going to Him, this would be perfection. But you invert the parts, and you love Him for His gifts, and you love His gifts for your own sake. So, you love Him for yourself, that is to say, you love yourself. You love the consolation of God; but do you love the God of consolation? You do not love the trial sent by God; but do you at least love the God who sends the trial? You love yourself, that is more or less all your heart can do.

And every morning and every evening you say to God, "My God, I love Thee with all my heart, above all things" — three lies. It is not really Him that you love, but yourself;

5. St Augustine, *Soliloquies*, I, 1. No. 22.

and if you love Him, even a little, it is certainly not with all your heart, nor really above all things. It is not good to lie to God like this and to lie to oneself, and to be content with words. Do you believe in God? Who should be first, you or Him?

So, your affections also are upside down; you love all things and God Himself in the opposite way to how you should. You are always first in everything you love. And you are a proud Christian! To love is to want the good. If you want the good of God, which is His glory, you love God. If you want your own good, you love yourself. When will you love God's good before yours? His honour more than your happiness?

You know that charity is superior to hope, and that without charity, hope is nothing. Hope is for you, charity is for God. When will you learn, with all truth and sincerity, to pronounce from the innermost depth of your heart a true act of love for God? "My God! I love Thee ... with all my heart ... above all things ... for love of Thyself ..."

XX   WHERE DO YOU STAND? (CONTINUED)

And what about your actions? You eat and drink to meet your needs, you amuse yourself for your pleasure, you speak for your own benefit, you work for your success, you come and go to serve your interests.

Your interests. You look for them everywhere, you pursue them without ceasing: and you can consider yourself very fortunate when they do not make you commit acts of cowardice! Self-interest causes many such acts to be committed. But here I am not talking about the evil you commit; I speak of the good you think you are doing, and in this good I see the quest for yourself dominating always and everywhere.

Is it not true that a human purpose usually inspires your actions? What you do ordinarily has a very clear and defined purpose. This purpose is some usefulness to yourself — natural and, sometimes, predominantly material usefulness — but this matters little; you are always first and the most important.

What place does God's interest hold in your conduct, compared to your own interest? Quite a narrow place, is it not? Too narrow, really — very secondary. I will admit that from time to time you know how to forget yourself, to make a sacrifice, to do all you can; but still, this is not exactly what has dominated your horizon so far. Yes, selfishness, even in doing good; even in doing one's utmost!

And what an influence the eye of man has over you! Does God's eye have as much influence? Is it not true that, in practice, you fear the eye of man more than the eye of God? There are many things you would not do if you were not seen, and others that you would not do if you were seen. Add up the number. The eye of man changes your behaviour in an extraordinary way; how does the eye of God change it?

So, in practice, since you have to be practical and try not to delude yourself, God means less to you than man, because He has less practical influence on the direction of your conduct. A Christian who believes in God must respect the eye of God alone, and never allow himself to be dominated by the eye of any man. As long as you feel that the eye of man alters the basis of your conduct, admit that God does not hold first place for you. As long as you are a slave to any human respect, even to that which makes you do good, your life will not have the righteousness it should have, and you will not behave in a way worthy of your faith.

A century ago, the French Revolution proclaimed the rights of man; and do we not put them into practice wonderfully? When will the rights of God be proclaimed again? And when will we return them to their place? The rights of God come before everything for him who has faith. Do you believe in God? Who should come first, Him or you?

Come, we must serve resolutely — serve God. You know that the Catechism says, "Man is created to know, love and serve God". Do you understand these three verbs — to know, to love, to serve? Do you understand this direct object — God? Do you know the Commandment, the one which is the greatest and the first? "Thou shalt love the Lord thy God, with thy whole heart, and with thy whole soul, and with thy whole mind, and with thy whole strength" (Mk 12:30). It is God Whom you must love and serve; and love and serve with your whole strength. God says specifically, "with thy whole strength". You know that God is not satisfied with words, and He is not in the habit of speaking so as to say nothing.

Once again, meditate on the great Commandment. Our Lord declares that He is the greatest; do not make Him the least. Declare that He is first, do not make Him second. The Commandment concerning your neighbour and yourself comes only second (Mk 12:31; Mt 22:37). So, once and for all, yield to your faith and to your reason, in order to keep these two Commandments in the order in which God placed them.

XXI STRAIGHTENING OUT

"But then, do I have to turn my whole life upside down?" — Yes, you have to turn it upside down, and straighten it out. Nothing more nor less is needed to overturn and straighten out the whole of your ideas, affections and actions. You see, love and act backwards, because you put yourself in the first place everywhere, and this is the great lie of your life. We need to make as our own these words, once and for all, "let us not love in word, nor in tongue, but in deed, and in truth" (1 John 3:18).

"So, must I stop thinking, loving and acting for myself?" — Who told you this? Let us go back to God's plan. God gave you a double purpose: His glory in the first place, your happiness in the second place. Since He gave you both, you are not allowed to suppress either of them. Right now, you suppress His glory too much; but this is no reason to go to the opposite extreme, and suppress your happiness. Keep to the plan of God: straighten things out, put things back in their proper places; that is a lot, and that is enough.

"Yes, a lot, and I am even afraid that it is an impossible job; a man cannot rebuild his own life as if it were simply turning his pocket inside out." — No, a man does not remake his life so quickly. But there is never a need to ask ourselves if this is impossible; this is the first and last argument of cowards. Leave to cowards their cowardice and their arguments. Are you not resolved to go all the way with your principles, and to be logical to the end? We must ask ourselves only if this is our duty, and duty is never impossible, even when it is necessary to sacrifice one's life for it.

What seems impossible to me is that you have faith, or, to put it better, that you have reason, and that you nonetheless continue to give God the place you have given Him in your life. Being logical with yourself, you will either fulfil your duty to the end, giving full and complete satisfaction to your reason and your faith, or else you will deny God, and then you will be free to talk nonsense; that is, you will lie to yourself, you will lie to your faith and your reason, you will live by expedients and half measures, you will be a useless and falsified man, your life will have neither logic nor truth, you will only be one vulgar juggler among many on the world's stage. You choose.

"But how can I undertake such a colossal work, which is nothing less than to re-found my life?" — Come on! Be a generous and sincere man, tell God that He can rely on you, and you on Him. Be resolute in everything, and you will see that God will direct you. You cannot imagine how simple this great work is. It all lies in knowing how to do it; but I will show you this later. The great Architect of this building can do everything, because, as you will see, this Architect is God.

Did you not see, at the beginning, that the supernatural life is a life in which God Himself makes the soul live, as the soul makes the body live? It is He Who makes you live for

Himself. You now live for yourself, because you live from yourself; that is, depending on your bodily and natural life. You will not live for God, until you live from God; that is, from that supernatural life in which God takes possession of your mind, your heart and your senses, to make you know, love and act supernaturally for His sake. You will therefore have to let God take possession of you, so that He can rectify your thoughts, your affections and your actions.

XXII   CURRENT CHRISTIANITY

And now examine the state of society. Look at where we are. On the one hand, there are implacable enemies of the Name of God, who strive in every way to remove the idea of God from all that is human. And you know how fierce the fight is, and what proportions it has taken. On the other hand, there are beings who believe themselves to be Christians, who call themselves Christians, who claim to work for God, and yet who leave Him only a very secondary place in the economy of their life. Do you understand the falsity of such a state of things, and the fatal nothingness to which one is condemned by being part of it? God is all or nothing: He is first or not at all; from the moment in which He is not in His place, He ends up with nothing.

Be careful: in private as in public life, in civil life as in politics, and even in religious life, does God really enjoy first place? Almost nowhere is He in first place. Self-interest dominates intelligence, subjugates hearts, and guides actions. Life is organised in such a way that man is put first in everything. The whole organism, from family to religious society, is distorted.

What is our education? Our formation? Our instruction? Our education should put God at the top of our mind; our formation should place Him at the centre of our heart; our instruction should place Him at the foundation of our conduct. What is happening now? Our education is human, our formation is human, our instruction is human. If room is made for God, this happens at an isolated shrine, where practical life hardly enters in. We make Him a more or less beautiful hut, in this hut we give Him a small part of our life, and we call this Christian life!

Neither in ideas, nor in morality, nor in laws, nor in institutions, nor in individuals does God have the place strictly due to Him. In short, everything is in great disorder; consequently, everything must be turned upside down. Do you now understand why socialists are necessary and inevitable? And it is we who claim to be good, above all, who make them necessary. When good itself is no longer right, there is no longer anything right and catastrophe is imminent, because society, like the individual, cannot live standing on its head.

If only we decided to stand up straight! If we reform ourselves instead of shouting at the dustmen who, after all, are only doing their job by taking away the rubbish; if we vomit up the revolutionary poison with which we are soaked to the marrow, if we learn to know, love and serve God, everywhere placing Him above man, we would do the only serious and necessary work in the present moment. Reform yourself, therefore, before committing yourself to making your contribution to some social work. Then you can carry out works that are righteous.

XXIII   THE AGES OF FAITH

In times in which there was faith, God had a very different place in life. The law of the first fruits consecrated to Him the firstborn of man, of animals and of the products of the earth. The first part of everything was for Him. Prayer and the sign of the cross were everywhere; the ordinary actions of life always bore a religious mark. Public and private acts were done in the name of the Father and of the Son and of the Holy Ghost. Nothing was done without God. If we spoke about a project, we said, "if it pleases God"; if we obtained a happy success, "thanks be to God" — beforehand, we relied on Him, afterwards He was thanked. Private and public life were oriented towards the honour of God. We were the servants of God. The peoples' most sacred interest was God's honour, and the most loathed crime was sacrilege.

Public legislation, peoples' customs, social institutions and popular ideas were marked by a profound religious imprint. Man had his passions and his sins; but above the human passions, the idea of God was seen to dominate everywhere. The great struggles, the great laws, the great ages, the great peoples, are those in which one sees the divine idea inspiring human activity.

The true history of humanity should be studied in the light of these principles: since history is nothing other than the knowledge of God's action in the midst of human unrest. And look at what you have learned in history. You have learned to follow the events of human unrest; but what have you learned from God's action? De Maistre is quite correct to say that for three hundred years history has been an incessant conspiracy against the Truth.

Christian society must be rebuilt; and, to rebuild it, the first thing which is required is to straighten out one's ideas. As long as we do not have upright ideas, we will walk wrongly, because man walks according to his ideas. It is the idea that makes the man. Today, there are no more men because there are no more ideas, there are only words. Do you want to be a man? Get away from words, and have ideas, that is, profound visions of things. And in order to have profound visions of things, it is necessary to see them as they are, and as God made them, and as they are guided by God. And to see them in this way, you need to place yourself in the point of view in which God wants you: when someone is in the wrong place, he sees falsely. So, God first and then you.

When you have implemented this great programme — God first in your ideas, in your loves, in your actions, in your whole life – then you will begin to be a Christian. — "How will I begin? For then, at least, I think that I will exist fully." — Not yet fully, for what I have just told you is only the first and not even the better part of the Christian life. There is still another, more beautiful, more extensive and deeper part. And if you believe in God, you are logically obliged to follow it to the end; I will teach it to you in the second part.

PART II

GOD ALONE

I MY GOD AND MY ALL

You have learned to put God in first place; and there He must be, because that is the place suited to Him; but is that enough for Him? If you believe in God, have you no other obligation to Him? Let us go back to the fundamental principle, since we must live by principles.

God created you. He created you for Himself. He created you completely: your being and all the parts of your being come absolutely from Him. You have nothing that does not come from Him. Could God have done what He has done for any essential purpose other than Himself? No. Your entire being as a whole and in its parts must therefore point to Him. Consequently, there must not be even the smallest part of your life that is not directed to Him. Creatures have no right to take up the least part of your vital movement. As long as any part of your being does not go towards God, but stops and rests outside of Him, you deny God's rights. As long as He is not your all, He is absolutely not your God.

Do you believe in God? What is there for you apart from God? Tools, nothing more than tools. He alone is your purpose, your goal, your end. Outside of Him, all that is created is a tool to move towards Him. How important it is for you to understand the significance of this word: "tool".

You know that we have agreed not to be satisfied with just words, and to get to the bottom of things. I have told you that this word has mysterious depths; now is the time to plumb them. Keep in mind this principle, which will seem to you as clear as daylight: the gifts of God are not God. St Augustine says that the gifts of God are the vehicle of God. In order to come to us and lead us to Him, God needs a vehicle. His gifts — that is, all creatures — are this vehicle. He uses them to come to me and I must use them to go to Him. Thus, creatures are, at the same time, God's tools and mine. He uses them, and I have to use them too, as we will see in Part Three.

It is so clear that one must not confuse the vehicle with the visitor and treat one as the other. When a friend comes to visit you, a vehicle brings him and you allow it to leave, while he stays with you. So, also, when you go to see a friend, you pay the driver, and you stay with your friend. You must do the same with God. You know that life is the journey of our return to God. We do not lack vehicles; why do we use them so poorly? We play around like children: we attach ourselves to the vehicle and pay very little attention to the visitor. We care about God's gift, and we care very little about His Name. His Name is He Himself; His gift is the creature. Truthfully, we are attached — attached to all creatures — and not at all attached to God. We care about His gifts, but very little about His Name.

When will you understand, and repeat the cry of St Francis of Assisi, "My God and my All"? The good saint spent whole nights in ecstasy, repeating these words alone:

"My God and my All". For him, everything was nothing; God alone was everything. For those who believe in God, this necessarily happens. He who knows Who God is, and what creatures are, he who does not allow himself to be fascinated and deceived by seductive appearances, sees and feels that God alone is his All, and says to God with the Psalmist, "For what have I in heaven? and besides Thee what do I desire upon earth? For Thee my flesh and my heart hath fainted away: Thou art the God of my heart, and the God that is my portion for ever" (Ps 72:24–25). When will He be your portion, your only portion? "My God and my All!"

II WHERE HAPPINESS IS

"But should we then love nothing?" — We must love all things for God. We must love things as we love a tool. Let us repeat the words of St Augustine: we must have them in our hands, not in our heart. — "But, in the end, may I not ask them for a crumb of happiness?" — Let me explain. If you believe that God is God then He is your All. For whom and for what did He create you? Will you do Him the injury of believing that He is not so great as to be enough for your happiness? "What will be enough for him, for whom not even God is enough?"[6] You are always reduced to the same choice: either denying God and lying to yourself, or recognising that He is God and, consequently, your All.

[6] St Augustine, *Sermons*, 1, 58, 9.

Yes, the happiness for which you are made — the purpose of the present life, as well as of the future — is found only in God. There are two things that sacred scripture recommends at every moment and in all moods: the first is to sing the praises of God, the second is to be happy. It repeats thousands of times the invitation to the just man to be cheerful. But it is not content with inviting to joy; it also says where to get it. "Be glad in the Lord, and rejoice, ye just" (Ps 31:11). Here is the one fount of the only happiness. From this source alone do the righteous drink happiness. Why do you go to drink elsewhere? That which you drink elsewhere is not the joy of the righteous, therefore it is the joy of evil.

III CREATED PLEASURE

"But then why did God place so many pleasures in creatures; pleasures in the beauties of nature, music and all the arts; pleasures of food, rest and entertainment; pleasures of relationships, friendship and prayer? God has sown them everywhere: were they not for us to enjoy?" — Now, this is also a very important question, and it is here that you will most closely touch the goodness of God and your own wickedness. Is it not true that when you have a good tool — well-made, easy to handle — you take pleasure in using it, and that, using it with pleasure, you accomplish better, faster and more easily that which you have to do? When it comes to an important job, tools are never too precise, perfect or easy to handle. It is difficult to do a good job with tools that you can handle only with difficulty.

God knows this. Therefore, in every tool He wanted to place a pleasure for you. For every duty there is a tool to accomplish it, and with every tool there is a corresponding pleasure in accomplishing the duty well. Do you understand the counsels of God and His goodness? See, then, the infinite considerations of His love. He entrusts you with a magnificent commission: that of glorifying Him and of making yourself blessed. For this, He gives you an infinite number of tools, which are creatures. To make it easier for you to use these tools, He places a pleasure in each of them: this is created pleasure.

So what is created pleasure for you, then? It is, to your faculties, what oil is for wheels. Consider a carriage. Try to move it when everything is dry and it is a useless effort. The friction creates too much resistance, the screeching is violent, the movements stunted, and the mechanism fails in a short time. Put a drop of oil in the most suitable places, and the friction ceases; movement is carried out with the utmost ease, the whole carriage works without failing. In order to act with ease and strength, even your faculties need a little oil; "the oil of gladness" that God has made specifically to lubricate, so to speak, the mechanism of souls who have "loved justice and hated iniquity" (Ps 44:8).

So, what is the function of created pleasure? It is that of facilitating your work; that of attracting, enticing, elevating, encouraging, expanding, fortifying your faculties in the exercise of your duty. It is therefore a pleasure in tools, a simple easing of work, and never an end in itself. Examine all pleasures: from the most supernatural to the most material; from divine ecstasies and consolations at the high peaks of perfection, to those of food and reproduction in the lower areas of the preservation of the individual and of the human species: their whole purpose, without exception, is to facilitate the fulfilment of a duty. A created pleasure, therefore, in God's conception — imprint this well in your head — is always a response to a duty to be accomplished. It is never given to you for amusement or to abuse it, but to use it. You are not made for it, but it is made for you. You, on the other hand, are made for God alone.

Hence, you see the misfortune of those who want to abuse pleasure and amuse themselves with it. They let themselves be fooled by it and forget about duty. What God had made only for facilitating duty, becomes instead its greatest obstacle. He who plays with spiritual consolations ends up losing all supernatural power; he who plays with sensual pleasures, alas, becomes a brute. It is a frightening thing to go outside the order of God! Every pleasure you want to enjoy and linger in becomes a real poison for your soul and body. Remember this: created pleasure is a remedy for external use only: woe to you if you swallow it! So, instead of swallowing it, use it; it will help you to do your duty. Use it externally; that is, according to the expression of St Augustine, hold it in your hand and do not allow it to lodge in your heart. Let pleasure only serve duty; never separate these two things.

Any pleasure, amusement, fun, joy or satisfaction that you separate from your duty ruins you. Fear, as you do, death; that is, fear pleasure that suffocates your faculties in the egoism of enjoyment. That which leads you to your duty, however — that which gives your faculties the impetus, the strength, joy, vigour, the agility to carry out your duty with ease and promptness — now that is indeed good and beneficial. God blesses it, so do not fear to make use of it. You do not have to destroy the good things that God has made, you have only to break the bad tendencies of your nature. See again how considerate God is in His goodness! In the beginning, He created only tools and not obstacles, pleasure and not suffering. Each creature was a tool, and each tool had its pleasure. Sin deeply upset this first plan of God; it changed a lot of tools into hindrances, and a multitude of pleasures into suffering. Obstacles and suffering are consequences of sin.

Even after sin, God's goodness to us has made Him find the means of turning obstacles themselves into tools, and suffering into joy. The Saviour's Passion worked this miracle. Everything serves the good of the elect; even the obstacles of sin. And everything becomes joy for them; even suffering, which becomes the greatest of joys.

IV HUMAN ABERRATION

How much wisdom and goodness there is in the counsels of God; and on the other hand, how much folly and wickedness in the behaviour of man! Greedy for happiness — and for a happiness without measure, because God made him for this — man turns to every creature in which he sees pleasure, reckoning that this pleasure is the purpose of his existence. "Does one not need to have a little happiness in life?" he goes about saying. And he seeks out and indulges the pleasures of the eyes, ears, smell, taste and touch. He makes the most sublime aspiration of his life consist in procuring created goods and pleasures to the greatest extent possible. He considers happy those who can possess and enjoy them, and unfortunate those who cannot. Such is the worldly and utilitarian concept of life. This concept dominates everywhere. A strange concept of life; a double aberration.

Undoubtedly it is licit to seek happiness: not only licit, but obligatory, since God wills it. But is this a reason to seek happiness where it does not exist, and to give this false happiness an importance it does not have?

Let us repeat: 1) happiness is not found in created pleasure; 2) happiness is not the highest aspiration of your life. You, however, go looking for happiness in created pleasure, and your first concern is to procure yourself a happiness that is false. Here is your double aberration. Do you not believe that putting creatures on the same level as God, and behaving as if He alone is not enough for your happiness, is to pay Him a great insult? Are you not splitting your faith in this way? If you believe in God, you must believe that He is your All, and that nothing is like Him: and you must not place anything on the same level as Him; and, apart from Him, nothing must be of essential importance to you, and you must use all things as tools, and "use this world, as if [you] used it not", says St Paul (1 Cor 7:31).

In the full light of faith, in the calm of your conscience, does it not seem abominable to you to overturn God's plan and to make that which He established only as a means the purpose of your life? Is this aberration not a monstrosity? Note that your aberration is not limited to this. In fact, it is this false, displaced pleasure, taken in a creature, that you ordinarily let come before the glory of God. The mere fact of attaching yourself to this pleasure outside of God is already a true perversion. What will it be like, when you prefer it to God? Calculate the depth and extent of disorder in your life.

You see that this evil has two immense levels. The first is to consider created pleasure as a purpose. The second is to prefer this pleasure to God. Consequently, there is a double work to do. First of all, it is necessary to prevent created pleasure from gaining the upper hand in your life; then you have to detach yourself from this pleasure, so as to reduce it to being nothing more than a means. So, what did I teach you in Part One? To put God in first place; this is, only to heal the essential part of the disorder, to prevent created pleasure from surpassing the glory of God. It can be said that I did not teach you anything else in Part One. Such an effort already seemed long and great to you. And so it is.

So, do you understand now that this first work is neither the longest nor the most difficult? Do you understand that God, while occupying first place for you, is still far from possessing it completely? You have to free your soul from all created pleasure to which it is falsely attached; this attachment must be broken. And this is a very arduous job; because your whole being, from the first of your faculties to the last, is infected with the charm of created pleasure. When you have completely corrected this part of your aberration, which makes you see creatures and their pleasures as something more than tools, then your purification will be complete, then you will be Christian, you will believe in God, your life will be composed of righteousness and truth, and you will live.

V   DETACHMENT

The first operation, indicated in Part One, is called "straightening out"; the second, which now needs to be studied, is called "detachment". Straightening out has placed God first; detachment will ensure that He alone will be your All. God first, this is the plan for the first part of the Christian life; God alone, here is the plan for the second part. It is at this cost that you will be a Christian: when will you be one? Are you determined to be one?

God alone! You see: they are just two little words; but they have a range of meaning that you and I are totally unable to measure. It is necessary to have attained a complete stripping to know exactly what these two words mean. The saints in heaven know this; but souls who come to know it in this world are very rare. In fact, it is rare to reach the summit of purification in this mortal life. Even if we cannot measure the distance that separates us from the summit, we can have a view wide enough to conceive some idea.

You believe in the Gospel? So do I. Well then, let us take Our Lord at His word. Let us not try to play His word down, because this would be a lessening of our faith. It is necessary to accept the Gospel in its entirety and in all its rigour; otherwise, we will be only false Christians, and what is the point of being false? You do not like fake products;

why would you want to be one? You have heard that saying of the Saviour in the Gospel: "If any man come to Me, and hate not his father, and mother, and wife, and children, and brethren, and sisters, yea and his own life also, he cannot be My disciple" (Lk 14:26,33).

This sentence of Jesus Christ is formal, absolute and most clear: one must detach oneself from everything and adhere to nothing but Him. He intentionally specifies the pleasure, which is the most honest, the most useful, the most invigorating of all — the pleasure of family, which is also the most usual, the best known and the most appreciated, the healthiest and the purest of natural pleasures. He uses it to label all the others. And He says that you have to give it up, along with everything you have — from the lowest pleasure, to life itself. Once again this is a formal order, and you must not think at all about changing the Gospel.

Note well that Our Lord says that we must hate, which means removal from the heart; removing the affections that dominate it, that oppress it. These pleasures must be removed from our hearts in order to be taken in our hands. It is not necessary to destroy them. The oppression that they exert over the heart must be destroyed. And that is precisely what the Saviour means by this word "hate". He does not forbid loving one's father, mother, etc. but He forbids such love to oppress the heart; He wants you to use this love as one of the best tools given to you to work for His glory, instead of feeding on it as a selfish enjoyment. Now, without a doubt, the ordered love of the family constitutes a very effective means for the soul who wants to use it to go to God. How many advantages derive from this for parents who want to raise their children well! How many advantages for children who want to be raised well!

As long as parents and children use this pleasure to progress in the practice of duty, all is well, because this is precisely what God wants. But when they abuse it for the sole satisfaction of loving each other, forgetting, neglecting or forsaking their duty for the sake of enjoyment, then it is bad; and it is precisely this that Jesus Christ condemns. Do you understand the Saviour's thoughts and words? Do you understand Christian detachment? Then have the same reasoning regarding all other pleasures, and you will learn how to use them for duty, and not abuse them for your satisfaction.

VI SLAVERY

"But, good God, the Christian life is impossible!" St Paul begins by warning us that, "if in this life only we have hope in Christ, we are of all men most miserable" (1 Cor 15:19). We Christians must strip ourselves of everything to find God alone. Our true life is an absolute stripping of that which is created, in order to enjoy only the One Who created us. In this world, we purify and expand, in order to live in eternity. So, we do not have our whole life in this world, we only begin and prepare it.

Besides, you must not believe this life to be impossible nor consider it to be so frightening. If it has its difficulties, it also has its joys; if it has its labours, it also has its benefits. It has fruits of sweetness that are not reserved exclusively for Heaven, and which are allowed to be enjoyed already in this world. Let me show you three of these fruits, of which I want you to savour the delights. The first comes from your relationship with yourself, and it is freedom of soul. The second arises from your relationship with your neighbour, and this is the blessing of true love and Christian dedication. The third comes from your relationship with God, and this is the incomparable sweetness of divine love.

The first fruit of the Christian life that I want to show you is freedom of soul. I believe that you know from experience that you are a slave to every pleasure that enters your heart. The pleasure that you feel you need is your master; it oppresses you and you cannot do without it. You know something about this, do you not? To be free again, you must draw this pleasure out of your heart, and take it in your hands, in order to be able to use it or put it away at will, according to its greater usefulness to you.

Now what does Christianity ask of you? Precisely this: to clear your heart, to be free; in other words, to throw out all created tyrants — that is, to reduce each creature to its simple function as a tool. So, is being free such a shallow thing? In these times when freedom has taken refuge under all sorts of banners because it is no longer found in souls, is it such a trivial thing to try to put it back in its place? Leave the freedom of public manifestos to fools, and work to have true, great, full and absolute freedom in yourself. "Rule," said the Master of all things at the beginning (Gen 1:28). After all, you must understand that Christian stripping is not a brutalisation and a suppression of everything but a liberation and taking possession of the tools of life. As long as created pleasure is in your heart, it dominates and possesses you. Without realising it sufficiently, you are now, more or less, the slave of all creatures. It is necessary, once and for all, to cease being possessed and to become the possessor. Until now, you have dragged your chain, so that you are left with only a very vague idea of the possibility of being able to live another way. You are so used to living as a slave, tossed about by your passions, your needs, all the seductions and unrest, that you no longer know what freedom is and are afraid of it, almost as a disgrace. So think about it! Do not join yourself to anything any more! Do not be attached any longer to any kind of shackles!

VII FREEDOM

Come, do not love your slavery, nor fear freedom so much. You believe that you are happy, attaching yourself to creatures, but look: how many involuntary separations, how many cruel tears, how many heart-breaking disappointments? The pleasure that you thought you held escapes you at every moment, and what you held most dear is violently snatched from you. These are terrible pains which bestrew the entire life of those who want enjoyment. They are lacerations of the heart renewed every second: divisions of interests, rivalries of self-love, conflicts of all kinds, losses of relatives, friends, money, position, esteem, and the infinite drama of disappointed passions. Here is a small idea of the delights of life experienced by those who attach themselves to created pleasure.

On the other hand, the Christian who cares for nothing never has his heart torn; he takes and leaves all things as easily as I take up and set down my pen. He is free from tyranny and sorrow. He uses everything, and he serves only God. Everything in the events of life is equal for him, because everything is a means for him. Nothing disturbs or discourages him because he is master of everything. Whether everything is given to him or taken away, it matters little to him; he conforms in everything to the good pleasure of the One Who gives and takes away, and blesses His Name (cf. Job 1:21).

Here is true freedom. Like St Paul, the Christian knows how to have abundance and knows how to deprive himself, he is used to everything (Phil 4:12). Come, you slave of self-love, you slave of foolishness, learn what freedom is: be a Christian. Health and sickness, pleasure and suffering, wealth and poverty, honour and contempt, friends and enemies, life and death, all serve the one who is detached from everything; he does not allow himself to be opposed or stopped by anything, because he is above everything. By disengaging himself, he is able to use everything as a tool. He is not seduced by pleasure, nor is he troubled by opposition.

He is the one who possesses constant equanimity and ignores the ups and downs — signs of the slavery from which he has escaped. His spirit is serene, his heart is at peace, his strength is focused; never pushed from one side to the other, his life is not wasted in the movements of false deviation. What a life! And what freedom! Does living as a Christian still seem such a scary thing to you? Do you still believe that this liberation from conflicts and oppression, from restlessness and divisions is so despicable? Unity and peace: this is the supreme result of freedom in the Christian soul. It is the first fruit I wanted to show you.

VIII   TRUE LOVE

"But will not this imperturbability, this freedom of heart, end up making humans insensitive, heartless and without love?" — Here it is necessary to make known the second fruit of Christian life, one which arises from your relationship with your neighbour and which consists in the beatitudes of Christian love and dedication.

You fear that you will no longer be able to love once you have acquired freedom and peace. Tell me, then, what do you mean by love? What does love mean in your opinion? I will tell you what love is for you: it is the pursuit of your pleasure. In your relatives, in your friends, in everything that is close to your heart, look closely: what you love is the excitement, the pleasure that comes from it. The proof of this is that, because of a disagreement, or because of sorrow, your love gives way with disconcerting ease to a bad mood, resentment, anger, hatred. You hate as easily as you love. It is enough for a simple appearance, a slight suspicion, to make you believe that your pleasure is upset, and the needle of your compass has already made a turn of the dial. You are faithful to only one thing, and that is your satisfaction. And this is what passes for love in the world.

The Christian has a completely different way of understanding love. If he loves his relatives and friends, it is for their sake, nor for his. He loves them in happiness and in misfortune, in setbacks as in joy, he loves them consistently and strongly. What his love seeks for them is their good and not their pleasure. For him, loving does not mean enjoyment, but doing good. The Christian thus loves everything with a strong and true love; his affection does not depend on the whims of his pleasure. His love faces sacrifices and privations, setbacks and enmities, "for love is strong as death, jealousy as hard as hell, the lamps thereof are fire and flames" (Cant 8:6).

Do not talk to me about those weathervanes that turn at every wind, about those hearts that are very easy on themselves and very hard on others. The Christian heart becomes inflexibly hard on itself, and exquisitely soft toward others. When you want to understand it, study the tenderness of the heart of St Francis of Assisi.

"But then, is there no more pleasure for the Christian heart?" — Say rather, "There is no more pleasure that deceives, annoys and misleads." Nothing that can dry up the marrow, atrophy the heart or mislead the spirit. But everything that can give vigour and strength, agility and ease, everything that can enlarge and elevate, purify and dilate, all of this enters the soul, and it uses it incessantly to develop its life. It does not enjoy sensations, external feelings and excitements, but the enlargement of its being. And since it is served by suffering for the expansion of its faculties, just as much as — and often even more than — by joy, it also knows how to enjoy suffering. The lie of your vain joys is found in their fleeing in the face of pain, like a flock of sparrows at a rifle shot; and, in the face of suffering, you are left with nothing but an empty heart, effeminate senses, a weak spirit. Desolation!

The Christian, on the other hand, does not lose any of his joys on account of pain, indeed it is often precisely then that he tastes them the most. Until your heart has felt a drop of that joy, which does not disappear in the face of suffering, you will not know what joy is. Believe me, it is worth being fully Christian if only to enjoy this drink. "Blessed are they that mourn," said the Master of the Beatitudes (Mt 5:5). Read all the Beatitudes; and when you begin to taste them, you will understand that the false joys which fascinate you are nothing but horrible deceptions. O heart, you that are made for such great things, stop letting yourself be suffocated by such childish trifles. The Christian Beatitudes are the second fruit of the Christian life.

The Beatitudes! The joys of the Christian life, which nothing disturbs, nothing alters, nothing destroys; not even suffering! Indeed, it feeds and increases them, O God, to what measure! When will you taste the Christian Beatitudes? Come, believe in Our Lord, believe in the Gospel! Believe that those whom Our Lord calls blessed in His Gospel must be blessed in reality. Believe it and try it. Listen: Our Lord and the Gospel already promise bliss for this world; and this, more than joy, is the summit of joy. If only you had faith!

IX ETERNAL BONDS

In chapter IX of Part One, you saw that all creatures are tools for you. Consequently, your relatives, your friends, your bosses and generally all men with whom you are in contact are tools for you. And the joy which governs all of your relationships with your neighbour is the same law which governs the use of creatures, according to which everything must be used as a tool. Did it not seem to you that this conception was too selfish and utilitarian? It will be good to show another depth here, that will bring you amazement and wonder.

You must understand first of all that, if others are tools for you, you too are a tool for them: reciprocity is absolute. If they are to serve you, you too must serve them. You must not only receive, you must also give: it is a mutual exchange. An exchange of what? An exchange of life; because one person can only be to another a tool of life. I do not know if you can glimpse the beauty of this idea. God does not put us in relationship with one another so that we all have fun together. Our relationships must legitimately have only one purpose: that of carrying out our life. And the joys of our relationships cannot legitimately have any other function than that of facilitating this development of life. Notice how much nobility and how much seriousness there is in this Christian conception of human relationships.

And look at the results also. At Montmartre, the stones bear the names of its benefactors; and will continue to do so as long as Montmartre remains. Your soul is the living temple of the living God; and your life is building itself every day, stone by stone, until the moment when death puts an end to the construction. The stones of this building are the ideas that your mind acquires, the virtues that are formed in your heart, the pure and strong habits that are established in your senses; and everything that expands your being according to the divine plan. And if I make you acquire a virtue, a growth in life, there is something of me in you, something of my life in yours, it is a vital bond that unites us.

As long as this growth, which comes from me, subsists in you, I will live in you in some way. Now, you know that life — I mean real life — is eternal. The life that I have communicated to you will subsist in the eternity of Heaven. We will therefore be united, united with the bonds of life, for all eternity. We will live through each other, in each other; this will be one of the splendours of eternal joy. Now think, how intimate and intense the happiness will be that will bind parents to their children, to whose upbringing they have entirely devoted themselves, those friends who were faithful in supporting and helping each other to climb! The more they have been tools of life for each other, the more they will live in each other. With what words can we recount the glory of the great sowers of ideas, of the great propagators of virtue, of the apostles of good, of men of sacrifice, who have been useful to so many souls, who have contributed to the expansion of so many lives? What bonds for eternity!

And this is the only thing that will exist of our temporal relationships. Imagine a family that lives in the enchantment of its selfish affections, imagine two friends who enjoy themselves in the pleasure of their friendship: they enjoy this together, and that is all that they look for. What will remain of these bonds? Alas, they have softened, weakened, atrophied together, and these relationships will only be punished by an eternal lessening. So, learn to live, learn to be a tool of life and to use all the joys of love for the good of others, through true zeal. When you know how to give such sublime grandeur to your relationships and your pleasures, when you know how to recognise and use the tools around you that will work on your own life, then you will no longer ignore the beauties of the Christian life so much. From now on, you will be able to taste something of the Beatitudes that you will fully enjoy in eternity.

X THE LOVE OF GOD

But, for the Christian heart, there is something infinitely superior to all this. You who want to enjoy the creature, will make yourself unable to enjoy God. You know that the alcoholic becomes insensitive to any taste other than that of alcohol. The same is true of you: as long as you seek out created pleasure, you will never be ready to taste divine pleasure. You do not know what God is and how sweet He is. Only to the extent that it is emptied does your heart become capable of tasting the sweetness of God — not the sweetness of His gifts, of His consolations, of His operations — no, but the sweetness of God Himself, of your union with Him, of your life with Him, of your possession of Him.

You know that the gifts of God are not God, but only the vehicle of God. When a distinguished benefactor, a close friend whom you have not seen in a long time, comes to see your family in a splendid carriage, you see the children hopping and ecstatic at the gilding of the car and the shiny harnesses of the horses. They do not think at all of the visitor, whom they do not know and who does not matter as much as that which shines in their little eyes. But the parents, moved, disregarding the elegant carriage and throwing themselves into the visitor's arms, take care of him, enjoy him, and are only happy with his conversation and presence. Tell me: of these two happinesses, which is the best? That of the parents or that of the children?

Up to now, you have been a child: you have toyed with the vehicle and you have as yet tasted only a few of the gifts of God. Try once and for all not to be a child: leave the vehicle and interact with God, and do not delay in understanding that it is better to be with Him than with His vehicle. Up to now, you have been able to delude yourself that you believe in God, love Him, serve Him and enjoy Him. But listen to me — your faith, your love, your service and your joy are but embryos. It is hard for you to have an idea of the greatness and beauty of the Christian life. God alone! Think carefully.

When you have tasted God, you will know what the third fruit of the Christian life is. And you will say with St Augustine: "Nothing that God promises to me has value without God. I would not be satisfied if He Himself, my God, did not promise me Himself. What is the whole earth, the sea, the sky, the stars, the sun, the moon? What are all the choirs of Angels? I thirst for the Creator of all these things, I hunger for Him, I thirst for Him. To Him I say: Thou art the Source of my life. Oh yes, hunger and thirst in my pilgrimage, in order to be satisfied in Thy presence. My God! I will not be satisfied, except when Thy glory is manifested."[7]

XI SEMI-CHRISTIAN

"But why are you calling me to such heights?" — It is not I who call you, it is God. Will you complain then that God has given you too great a destiny? Will you complain that I, for my part, do not allow you to scrape out a commonplace existence, and ignore your destiny? Yes, I want to tell you how great you are in God's conception, I want you to see to what height He calls you; I want to open before your eyes that infinite horizon for which you are made; I want every pettiness to be inexcusable in you. Since the beginning, I have asked you, "Are you determined to go all the way? Are you resolved not to stop on the way?"

What? Would you be cowardly enough to allow yourself to be only half a Christian? Never! Let us see: do you like things half done? If your tailor brought you a half-made suit, would you accept it? What good can half-made things do? You like to always have good and well-finished things, the fruits of your gardens, the furniture in your house, your servants, your friends; you want everything to be as perfect as possible. There is nothing, not even your shoes, that you do not want perfectly finished. Yet would you like nothing more than semi-perfection for your soul? "Tell me," says St Augustine, "will you not prefer your soul to your shoes?"[8]

[7] St Augustine, *Sermons*, 158, 7.
[8] St Augustine, *Sermons*, 232, *On the Resurrection of Christ according to St Luke*, 8.

"Yes, of course, I am absolutely determined to prefer my soul to my shoes; to want its perfection, its entire perfection. Yes, I desire and wish to go as far as God desires and wants. I will be a Christian without restrictions or lessening, a Christian all of a piece and nothing but a Christian. The sacrifices matter little; with the grace of God I will not be afraid. I thank my Creator for making me so great, and I thank Him for letting me know it now, because I did not know it before. Glory to God! It is He Whom I desire; He Whom I wish to know, He Whom I want to love, He Whom I want to serve, and in the measure that He wills." Yes, glory to God! Boldly take this ancient war cry as your motto. "God does not die", as was often said by that hero, who was such a Christian and who knew how to die for Him Who does not die. If only you had the faith of García Moreno! Believe in God, but in such a way that He is not only first, but All in your life. Glory to God! God does not die!

XII EXTERIOR STRIPPING

It is therefore necessary that you strip yourself of everything that stops you and prevents you from going to God. Now there is a double stripping: an exterior one and an interior one. The former frees you from the oppression of exterior things, the latter from the oppression of yourself. Do you want to learn how this stripping is done? First of all, the exterior stripping: you know that you are mind, heart and senses. The stripping must be done successively in these three orders of faculties, beginning with the lower: first, you have to free the senses.

To free the senses from external seductions, God sends you emotional consolations, the purpose of which is to progressively detach the emotional part of your being and remove it from the influence of exterior pleasures, to bring it back to Him. These consolations last as long as necessary, so that the exterior pleasure is overcome, and your senses are attached to God. But, mind you, this consolation is not God but is only the vehicle of God. If you cling to it, you will disturb and hinder God's operation to unite you with Him, and not with His vehicle. You have to know how to use it, and try not to enjoy it, in order to rest in it. So, when your senses are sufficiently detached from the outside, and the vehicle departs, all sensible consolation disappears. You will then be prey to dryness, and at that moment you will be able to see to what extent your senses are attached to God and free from emotional pleasure.

Aridity will be succeeded by great lights, profound visions of faith, knowledge of mysteries. These are powerful illuminations destined to conquer your intelligence, to detach it from exterior objects, to fix it in God. You understand very well that this is a new vehicle of God, the one by which He comes to your mind. But it is nothing more than a vehicle; you need to know how to use this too, without constraining your heart. These lights will last until they have conquered your mind; then they will disappear, and you will fall into darkness. Why this darkness? So that you can fully realise what your mind has attached itself to, whether to God or to His vehicle.

The period of darkness will be followed by a period of great fervour. Your heart will feel inflamed with immense desires for virtue and sacrifice, it will have such bursts of generosity that it will feel capable of sacrificing the whole world, to give all of itself to the love of God. Do you understand what these bursts are? They are the third vehicle of God, the one which comes to seek your heart; it will be at your disposal until your heart is completely conquered by God. But it will in turn have to disappear, and your heart will again find itself cold and helpless. This coldness will be the test by which you can verify if your heart is truly attached to God.

These are the three degrees of exterior stripping. Their operations are long and varied; because there are many exterior objects from which it is necessary to detach the senses, the mind and the heart! But believe this: such operations will be all the easier the better you know how to make use of consolations, lights and ardour, and the less you attach yourself to them. Use them and do not get attached to them, this is the fundamental rule, and these are the conditions for progress and advancement.

After these operations the soul becomes indifferent to pleasure, no longer dominated by anything else but duty. What it does from then on it no longer does for the enticement of pleasure, but for the attraction of duty. It is the idea of duty, the idea of the glory of God to be promoted, which dominates it, possesses it and leads it in everything.

So, it has a prodigious facility to do everything it can to contribute to God's honour.

This is the secret of the power of action exercised by the saints. Our nothingness comes from our pride. We want to enjoy ourselves and we make ourselves useless in this search for ourselves, and everything that we throw into this chasm of selfish enjoyment we make useless. Oh, the power of a soul that seeks nothing for itself, but everything for God!

XIII   INTERIOR STRIPPING

This is the great work. For if it is a great and difficult thing to renounce exterior things, it is even more difficult to renounce oneself. However detached you are from exterior things, you are not yet entirely detached from yourself. Complacency in your faculties and actions is far from being destroyed. Now, it is not in you but in God that you must be satisfied, as God must be your only All.

It is necessary, then, for God to tear away from your senses, from your mind and from your heart all complacency in yourself; you understand very well that these egotistical returns to yourself are not for Him. Therefore, here are the new operations that are necessary on the part of God.

He begins with the purification of the senses; and to detach you completely, He shakes them with horrible storms of pride, anger, impurity, jealousy, and others; so that the last leaven of evil may come out. Then He turns to your mind and shakes it in unspeakable darkness — in the anguish of doubt and uncertainty — until it is as dead to itself, and all selfish knowledge is banished, and God's will alone occupies it.

Then it is the turn of the will. God first takes away all power of action; the soul keeps only one power, that of suffering: it suffers and it accepts its suffering. Soon, it will no longer even have the energy to accept this; it will have nothing, no strength, no movement of its own. And then every separate and selfish movement of the heart will be suppressed. Nothing is left that is not united with God; the purification of the soul is complete, it is the perfection of the Christian life: the individual is all of God, all in God and all for God.

If one day or another, you have the happy opportunity to read well-written lives of the saints — I especially recommend the lives written by the saints themselves — you will find in them this series of operations and you will see their terrifying length. How spoiled our poor nature is, and what work it takes to restore its primitive integrity and righteousness! Now do you understand the meaning of those words of the Catechism: "Man is created to know, love and serve God"? Do you understand the extension of the Commandment that tells you: "You will love the Lord your God with all your mind, with all your heart and with all your strength"? This is how far that Commandment goes, which is the first and greatest of all. God demands everything and you will not have given Him this everything, until the moment you reach the last peak. Words also have a profound meaning when one has the will to measure it! And when God speaks to man, he gives to His expressions all the fullness of which they are susceptible.

Yes, meditate on the Great Commandment: "You will love" — that is, you will seek the good. Whose good? God's good, His glory; that is how you will love Him. "You will love the Lord your God"; you will love Him because He is, above all, your Lord — that is, your Master — and consequently, you have to put Him first. Then you will love Him as your God — that is, your All — and so you must strip yourself of everything and keep Him alone. "You will love the Lord your God". How will you love Him? "With all your mind"; your cognitive faculties must all belong to Him. "With all your heart"; your will power must belong to Him. "With all your strength"; your operative faculties must all belong to Him and serve Him. You were created solely to know, love and serve God.

XIV PURIFICATION AND GLORIFICATION

Pay close attention to this. In the interminable journey of the Christian life, which extends from the flight from mortal sin to the consummation in God, the work is always twofold. There is a work of purification, which drives out evil, and a work of glorification which expands and ennobles the soul. Without sin, there would have been only one work: that of glorification. All the vital energies that are in us and all those that come to us from God would have been concentrated on this single point of the expansion of our life. And what a life!

Now many of these energies are absorbed by sin; because every time you commit a fault, it dissipates a more or less considerable part of your vital energy. And to emerge from this guilt, a certain amount of energy is still required. So, the fall consumes something of your life, and getting up again consumes another part of it. If you had not fallen, you could have walked a long way on the same amount of energy. So, you see how deplorable it is to destroy one's life in this way.

Come, swear to God never to let yourself be dragged one step lower than where you are now. No doubt you already have enough work to do to climb back from where you are. The purifications that must take place in you are already enormous enough. Why do you want to increase their number? Since you feel within you the need to live, do not suffocate your life, especially when you see an infinite horizon wide open before you. Observe one more thing. The successive stages of your Christian development are measured, not from the positive side of glorification, but from the negative side of purification. In fact, it would be impossible for me to tell you, and impossible for you to know, to what degree of merit and glory you must reach.

Where do you stand? What progress have you made? Where do you still have to go in order to correspond with the universal plan of God, and to the absolute capacity of your being? God alone knows, He alone measures; because He alone knows the complete plan of your life and the true place that He allocates for you in the Body of His elect. Adore His secret and let yourself be led by Him to the height to which He calls you. But, on the negative side of purification, you can calculate your progress very well; and if you look carefully, it is from this side that I am trying to show you the ascents of the interior life. Observe how, in fact, the work of purification is carried out progressively through the escape from mortal sin, venial sin and imperfection, as I showed you in the first part. Then come the further purifications — that is, exterior and interior stripping — as I have showed you in this second part.

So you see, your absolute purification is accomplished in five degrees. According to this measurement, you know exactly how far you have to go, and it is not too difficult for you to know where you are, what you have done and what remains to be done, the degrees covered and the degrees left to go.

XV   PURGATORY

"What? Is it absolutely mandatory to reach to the top of this ladder?" — I could answer you that God was truly at the top of Jacob's Ladder — "the top thereof touching heaven" (Gen 28:12–13) — and that the same happens here, but it is good to distinguish again between the two operations of purification and glorification. Purification must be the same for everyone; that is to say, absolute; since you know that nothing stained can enter Heaven. As long as the most imperceptible trace of imperfection remains to be purified in the soul, it is absolutely impossible to enter Heaven. That is why, for the souls in whom the essential purification from mortal sin has at least begun in this world, Purgatory will accomplish to the last what remains to be done.

"What? My God! Everything? Everything ... until the very end? In Purgatory?" — Yes, without any remission or exception, purification must be absolute; what has not been accomplished in this life will be finished there. In this way you can understand how few souls enter Heaven directly when they leave this world, and why the Church, with so much effort and at such length, makes people pray for the dead. But glorification will not be the same for everyone. Each will keep in eternity the degree of development that he has acquired in his mortal life. He will stay at the point in which he dies, because the work of glorification, the expansion of the soul and the acquisition of merits do not continue beyond the grave but end when life does. Consequently, Purgatory is nothing but full-strength purification, with no other advantage except this same purification. See how important it is for you to work as much as possible in this world, for down here, the two operations always go hand in hand. One grows as one purifies oneself. And this growth is eternal; that means a greater capacity for glory and, consequently, greater praise for God, and greater happiness for you for all eternity. Come, do you believe in God? Do you believe in your religion? Do you have faith? It is time to show it in your works.

XVI   A PHILOSOPHICAL SUMMARY

Why do I appeal to your faith? To convince you of it. Would it not be enough to appeal to your reason? Do you admit that God is your Lord and your God? Your reason does not allow you to doubt it for a moment. If He is your Lord, you owe Him first place. If He is your God, He is your All. What would a lord be, if his servant could relegate him to where he liked? What would a god be that was not everything for his creature? Just try to get an idea of this. A lord who is put under your feet; a god who is but a half, a quarter, or even less! This overturns any idea of order and common sense.

Therefore, whenever you do not give your Lord first place, you are being unreasonable; and until your God is your only All, you remain unreasonable. That happens quite often to you, does it not? Being unreasonable. Have you been completely reasonable even once in your life? Only the saint who has truly reached the top is completely reasonable. If only you were reasonable to the extent that it is possible for you to be so! If only you did what is possible for you, by giving your Lord His due place every day, and giving your God the part that belongs to Him!

It is not good to lie to oneself, to lie to one's reason, and to lie to one's faith. It is all or nothing. Since you will never be an atheist, be a Christian — a Christian consistent to the end with the principles of your reason and your faith. Yes, reason itself tells you that, since God is your Lord, you must know Him, love Him and serve Him, first and for the sole reason that He is your Lord, that is, your Master. Yes, reason itself tells you that, since God is your God, you must know, love and serve Him alone, and for the sole reason that He is your God, that is, your All. God first, God alone: reason proclaims and wills it. And when everything that faith says is added to reason, what are you waiting for to become a Christian once again — a man of reason and faith?

Do not let yourself be stopped by the fearful tremors of nature which exaggerate difficulties, and do not know sweetness. God is God — that is, He is the highest good — your life is in Him, and your happiness too. Do not be afraid. Does the sick person fear health? Is the traveller afraid of his homeland? Besides, you will see further on how sweet the healing is, how easy the journey is. Certainly, these principles seem hard to you (cf. John 6:61). All principles are hard in themselves, hard for the whims of man, which they break; hard for the passions, which they oppose. But if you only knew that salvation lies right there! If you only knew how soft this hardness becomes and how much strength this rigour communicates! I beg you, be a man of principles; it is the only way to be someone and to do something.

XVII   THE SAINTS OF GOD

To what height the saints have risen! Undoubtedly, not all of them have done the full work of their purification down here. In some there may be some part left to do in Purgatory. But many reached the highest peak in this life and entered Heaven at the moment of their death. And as for those in whom a small part of the work was left to do, they had nevertheless travelled the path to its greatest extent. It goes without saying that they had fully carried out the first part of Christian life — God first — and also that they were already far ahead in the second — God alone. This is why they are so great! They had faith and reason, and they lived according to their faith and reason.

They were sincere men who knew how to renounce lies. They were strong men and did not consent to bargain with cowardice. There is no lie in their life because their conduct never lied to their principles. There is no cowardice because, if they had their weaknesses, they did not drag themselves down into discouragement and lethargy. They knew how to walk without letting themselves be disheartened by the infirmities of the flesh and the accidents of the journey.

They were men like you, with the same passions and nature, as well as with the same reason and faith. And they knew how to rise above their passions, to live according to their reason and faith. They were men! Pilate, showing Jesus Christ to the people, said, "Behold the Man" (John 19:5). And the Church showing her saints to the world, says, "Behold the men!" And will you be a man? A Christian? A saint? Do you have faith? Reason? Answer.

XVIII   THE BLESSED VIRGIN

You love your good Mother and, reading the preceding pages, you have instinctively raised the gaze of your heart to her, so as not to despair of yourself. How pleasing these looks are to me, and how beneficial for you! To encourage you even more, I want to show you, in the light of these principles, the greatness of that Mother whom you love so much.

You have become somewhat aware of the heights of the Christian life. Well, tell yourself that the Blessed Virgin was placed at these heights from the very beginning of her existence, through the privilege of her Immaculate Conception. In her, purification was absolute: in her mind, in her heart, in every sense. And she never emerged from it, and never was the slightest movement touched by a trace of imperfection in her whole life. Everything that was in her went to God alone. She did not have to carry out the work of her purification, since this was complete from the beginning, but worked only on that of glorification, without intermittence, without variation, without hesitation. What a life! What merits! And what greatness!

And yet this is but the small side of her greatness; I will show you the great side of it in Part Three, and I hope that your veneration and trust in her will no longer have limits, and that you will entrust to her maternal power the care of leading you on the great path of the Christian life. The good Mother is so elevated! She is so pure! And she has so much pity for poor sinners, whom filth keeps so far from God! By the privilege of her immaculate purity, she has the power of attracting souls who need to stand up. You feel this need; you feel in your heart the desire to live on the heights. Trust in Mary; a trust without limits. She extends her motherly hand to you, she looks at you with her eyes full of mercy, she encourages you with her all-compassionate voice. She who suffered so much for you opens her heart to you.

You know how much she loves you, or rather you do not, because she loves you more than you can imagine. She has a very ardent desire to see you close to her, pure like her, free from sin like her! Trust in her, and no height is inaccessible to you with her help. If only you knew how to pray to her! If you could put your hand in hers, your heart in hers! If only you were determined to walk!

Yet from your Mother, who is so great — who would like to make you so great, and to this end, would like to give you such great things — you ask for nothing but small things. You ask her for health, success, a place, consolation; and for all I know, sometimes even for a little virtue. Have you thought to ask her, with the absolute sincerity of a child's heart, for holiness? Yes, for holiness, which means a Christian life. This is what your Mother would like to give you; and to obtain this great treasure, she would give you everything else as a means. Will you ask her for this sublime gift — sincerely, resolutely, relentlessly? Come and look at your Mother; do not be content with words and do not lie to yourself anymore.

XIX JESUS CHRIST

But the One on Whom you must have your eyes fixed — "the author and finisher of faith" (Heb 12:2) — is Jesus Christ, Who is the Son of God made man. In Him, God is united to man by a perfect, indissoluble, personal union. He is the true summit of holiness. In Him the union of man with God was consummated in all possible perfection. And it is He Who makes Christians and saints. It is from Him, from the name of Christ, that the name of "Christian" derives. To be a Christian means to be made in the image of Jesus Christ, to be incorporated into Him, to receive life from Him and, through Him, to fully grow into divine life.

He came among us, lived our human life; giving us the model to follow in the examples of His life, and the rule to fulfil in the words of His teaching. It is to Him you must look; it is Him you must study if you want to become a Christian. You should know His life and His teachings by heart. Read, read the holy Gospel; do not stop drinking from this source the true spirit that must animate your life.

How can you flatter yourself to be a Christian if you know Our Lord Jesus Christ so little and so badly? You study chemistry and philosophy, which are not bad — they are useful to know and I enjoy seeing you study them seriously — but tell me, what place does the study of Jesus Christ have in the order of your occupations? Is this not something that you know less deeply? Have you read the Gospel at least once in your life? You have, no doubt, read many novels, but the Gospel? O so-called Christian! You do not know to what extent the title you carry is a lie. O Christian who does not read the Gospel, who does not know it, who does not make it the main object of his studies; and you believe in God? You believe in Jesus Christ? Then, once again, put your actions into agreement with your beliefs. Do not have dead beliefs, like herbs in an herbarium. Belief which is not transfused into practical life is nothing but a deceitful curiosity.

But Jesus Christ came, not only to live for us, but above all to die for us. He came to repair and to atone for our transgressions. And with the sufferings of His life and the pains of His death, He atoned for our crimes and washed away our filth. He redeemed us and brought us back to God.

The virtue of His Blood purifies and strengthens us, and communicates to our sufferings the power to merit and to make expiation. Our sufferings, combined with those of the Saviour, become immense treasures of sanctification. Therefore, as Christians, the Cross stands everywhere before our eyes and shows us that, wherever in life we encounter pain, the Cross of Jesus is there to sanctify it, transform it and give it divine merit.

Life with Jesus! But above all, suffering with Jesus! The great secret of great Christians! Learn what Jesus Christ is. Learn what His Cross is and you can call yourself a Christian, and anyone who meets you will be able to say: "Now, that is a Christian!" If only you believed in the sufferings of Him Who is your God and Who wanted to become a man like you in order to die for you! But you do not meditate on them enough, and therefore they have no effect in your life. Distracted Christian, the smallest curious news has more power over you than the death of your God. Would you fear sacrifices so much if you sincerely believed in the sacrifice of the Cross? Would your generosity be so apathetic and lazy if you understood the generosity of Jesus Christ? It is sad to hear that people believe in such sublime things, while their actions are so meagre. I beg you, have faith, and put your life on the level of your faith. Do you think that your God was constrained to come and suffer and die for you? If so, what would constrain Him to do it? Love! He loved you and died for you. You say to Him, "My God, I love Thee"; and yet you do not know how to live for Him! And yet you must live for Him; this is your duty.

If only you understood the crucifix! If only you understood these words expressed by the Cross: "Love! Give yourself! Do all you can! Sacrifice yourself!" Place yourself, once and for all, before your crucifix and ask Him Who lived and died for you to know how to live for Him. To live, that is to say, to give yourself, to do all you can, to sacrifice yourself; in a word, to love. Learn to be a Christian at the foot of the Cross.

PART III

WORK

I THE WORKERS

So far, I have explained to you the great principles which must illuminate the path of your life and guide your passage. You know what you are, and you know where you need to go. Are you not great in God's plans and desires? Are you not called to climb high? In this lies the greatness of the Christian, and the height of the Christian life.

How many times, measuring such heights, have you felt a thrill, thinking about the path to follow and the work to be done to get to such a height? It is time to encourage you and show you that, if the height is infinite, the path is smooth and the work is easy. The Master of holiness said: "Come to me, all you that labour, and are burdened, and I will refresh you. For my yoke is sweet and my burden light" (Mt 11:28,30). For my part, I believe in the Gospel, and I am convinced that everything Our Lord has said is true. You who are a Christian, and wish to be one even more intensely; do you believe in the Gospel and in all that it says? Oh, certainly you believe it. Well, the Gospel tells you that the Christian yoke is sweet and that its burden is light. So, why these restless fears about the work to be done and the pain to be endured? These fears are not Christian; they are lies to your faith, and contrary to the Gospel.

Let us therefore see how the work must be done, and how to see it; let us first ask ourselves, "who must do it?" I answer immediately: "God and you." God reserves His part of the work to Himself, and reserves yours for you. And if I were to ask, "which is the most important part, God's or yours?" then you would not hesitate to answer me, "God's". And if I added, "what is the work that must have first place, God's or yours?" then you would not hesitate to answer me, with all the more reason: "God's". Yes, God's work is more important than yours, and must be placed before yours. This is everything I want to show you in this third part. When you have learned to conform your own work to God's and to unite it with Him, you will understand the practice of the Christian life. But let us first see what God's work is.

II THE GENERAL ACTION OF GOD

What is the work of God? What does He do? Through His Providence He directs the universal activity of things, creating and sustaining them. He made all things to some purpose and directs them towards that purpose. You know that they are tools: tools of God, first of all; tools that He uses, since He is the Author and the One Who orders the innumerable activity of beings. You see the activities of the physical world, those of the moral world and, I scarcely dare add, those of the supernatural world too; perhaps you see these less, but we must learn to see them better.

All activity is connected, coordinated and oriented, with the same precision, as the very complicated movement of the different parts of a machine. You hardly know this connection at all, but you have to get to know it. Finally, all this activity must obtain a result: the same that is willed by God and in view of which He maintains it. And the final result that it must achieve is the perfecting of His chosen elect: not just general perfection but the perfection of each one individually. In fact, His wisdom is so skilful as to make all things contribute to the general good, as well as to the individual good.

The wisdom of the wise does not go so far. They see the fixity of physical laws, but they ignore the connection that these have with moral laws, and they do not understand the final purpose of created activity. So their vision is continually clouded by what seems to them an inconsistency, and the last word of their science is coincidence ... "Coincidence"! A word as empty of meaning as it is of faith. It is one of those fallacious words by which ignorance tries to deceive itself, and which bad faith abuses to blaspheme and deny its own action.

Since you want to be a Christian — and one of the utmost seriousness — I promise that you will later make some wonderful discoveries in this regard. If, until now, your view of this horizon has been closed to you because of your too superficial life, you will learn from now on to penetrate the mysteries of God's action, and I assure you that they are wonderful mysteries. The saints, who are the true visionaries, are in constant ecstasy, contemplating such hidden wonders. They see the coincidences and connections, the continuation and the opportuneness of everything. They see how creatures are the tools of God: for a single purpose, which is the making of saints. "And we know," says St Paul, "that to them that love God, all things work together unto good, to such as, according to his purpose, are called to be saints" (Rom 8:28).

Thus, physical and moral activity has a purpose and an outcome, to which it is coordinated and adapted. He who ignores this purpose, and the outcome which must follow, can understand nothing about this business of activity. When you place yourself in the centre of a circle, you see all the rays coming at you in a straight line; none are cut or broken. As soon as you move, the lines are immediately confused, broken, cut; none of them seems to be a straight line anymore, except for the single line along which you have moved. Are the rays actually less convergent than before? No, rather only your range of vision has changed: and everything seems false to you because of your false position.

To see rightly, you have to get to the right point; and you will not be at the right point unless you have truly reached the summit of the Christian life; until that moment there will always be something which appears false and incomprehensible to you. Nonetheless, as you advance towards this summit, you will see each day how new arrangements of God become clearer due to the righting of your position.

III THE SPECIAL ACTION OF GOD IN YOU

But what does God do for you in a special way? First of all, He created you; "Know ye that the Lord he is God: he made us, and not we ourselves" (Ps 99:3). He made you as

He wished, giving your body and soul the qualities and constitution that He liked. He gave you birth in the conditions
of the environment and time that He wanted. He Himself
drew up the laws of your physical, moral and intellectual
development and the laws of your supernatural growth. He
gave you a certain measure of being, a certain number of
faculties, a certain dose of inclinations. He gave your life
a certain direction, prepared you to take up a determined
position, a special function. In a word, He regulated all the
conditions of your birth and your vocation.

And how did He do this? By means of the tools that He
used. Of which tools? Of all the creatures which contributed
to the fact of your existence. Add up the number: first, your
parents; then the influences of time, air, food and all the
elements. How many things concurred in your birth! And all
these things were tools of God, set in motion and directed
by Him in order to give you birth in the conditions that He
wanted. And now that your life is developing, think a little
about the multiple influences under which it grows. How
many creatures come into contact with your body, with your
heart and mind! The physical influence of time, seasons,
climate, of all material elements, with their variations at all
times. The moral influence of your relatives and teachers, of
your friends and enemies, of the known and unknown men
whom you meet, of the events that take place, of the words
you hate, of the facts you see, of the conditions you endure;
the spiritual influences of grace, inspirations, temptations,
religious teachings, etc. What do I know? Thousands and
thousands of different touches, which act in the various
parts of your being.

So, what are all these influences, movements, touches? They are God's work in you. All these creatures are set in motion by Him, and they do nothing but what He wills them to do. You see that it is an incessant and extremely complex work. It is incessant, because you exist ceaselessly in relation to a mind, heart and body, with an infinite multitude of beings which act on and react to you. It is extremely complex, and you would be absolutely unable to analyse the details, calculate the number and know the chain of events. Besides, you are not required to make this calculation; God has reserved this to Himself. And you know — or maybe you do not — that He performs this calculation. He does it with an exactness that belongs to Him alone. You must see that what God calculates is admirably calculated.

Now, do you want to know to what extent the details of your life are calculated by Him? Ask Our Lord, and He will tell you, "But the very hairs of your head are all numbered" (Mt 10:30) — "and not one of them shall fall on the ground without your Father" (v. 29). So, if the number and loss of your hair is entirely calculated, what will not be? Nothing is insignificant to God, because He uses everything. If you were less blind, if you understood God, nothing would be insignificant for you: you simply do not understand. You have short-sighted faith.

So, everything that happens to you, everything that touches you, is calculated by God: why and how? In view of the development of your life in all respects. God knows how your life must unfold, because He drew up the laws. Now, it is in view of this progressive development that He arranges, in regular succession, the movement of the beings which act about us. Everything happens at a given moment; it acts exactly on the point to be developed, produces exactly the activity which is necessary. And, as long as you do not destroy this action of the elements, guided by the hand of God, your life expands with all the perfection to which God calls it. I say, "so long as you do not destroy it", because you have the frightening power to disrupt God's action by your own will!

You cannot imagine what a mystery of life is hidden in you; the circumstances of your existence include everything that you believe. One might rightly say that everything in you that you do not do yourself is done by God. He has tools, because everything is a tool of God. But if it is He Who does it, does your reason and faith allow you to believe that it is done badly; without purpose, without order and without counsel? Come now, look a bit more closely and recognise the infinite goodness of this God, Who incessantly takes care to arrange and order creatures for the good and the growth of your life. How beautiful is this mystery of love! And how life thus appears as something really vital! How divine are all its traits!

God knows when you need to be encouraged, consoled, strengthened, and provides you with joys and consolations as needed. He knows when you need to be shaken by jolts which will purge your dross, prove you by trial, sanctify you by expiation, detach you by sacrifice; and, for this purpose, He arranges the action of the creatures which try you. Men and animals, physical elements and moral events: from the bite of a fly to a supernatural inspiration; everything works in you according to God's plans! If only you knew how to believe in God and in His action!

IV SUPERNATURAL ACTION

You may find it difficult to believe that events have such a connection and such a meaning. Until now, you little suspected that external illusions could, deep down, be so vital to you! This is one of the misfortunes of your superficial life, to which it is time now to put an end. But here is something more wonderful still: the connecting of the supernatural order to the natural order. Every creature — spiritual or material, small or large — which acts in you, evokes an impulse from your faculties. In this way, there is an action exercised within you: an intellectual, moral, or physical action, exercised over your mind, heart, or senses. Do you know what is contained in this action? Nothing other than actual grace.

This grace is called "actual" because, on the one hand, it is the fact of an action exercised in you and, on the other hand, it pushes you to action by the very fact of the impulse that it contains. — "But then actual grace is everywhere!" — Yes, everywhere: there is nothing absolutely and exclusively natural in your life as a Christian; the natural is intimately and constantly linked to the supernatural. Let us repeat the picturesque expression of St Augustine: "The natural is the vehicle of the supernatural."

Here, already, is a part of the great mystery of the Incarnation. You know that Our Lord Jesus Christ, Son of God, united Himself with our human nature "to re-establish all things" according to the word of St Paul (Eph 1:10). How did He re-establish them? By making all things the tools of His grace, so that all things can impart it to men. Everything that God does in the world imparts His grace. Creatures are tools. You see these tools acting, moving, working. By whose hand are they set in motion? By the hand of God. What work do they do? They bring grace. Can you doubt, therefore, that the supernatural world touches the natural activity of beings from two sides? On the one side, God Who directs with His Providence; on the other, actual grace, which is the final result of the activity; tools act between both one and the other. This is the truth about the economy of the relationships of beings.

"How many graces there are, then!" — Oh, yes, how many graces! For they are everywhere; God acts continuously, in fact, and with every kind of tool. See how great your ignorance has been until now. You have contemplated the comings and goings of life, almost like a child listening to the tick-tock of a clock. The noblest interest you found therein was that of curiosity, but you have not cared to see God acting, and the grace which comes from this divine action. Do you understand that the true meaning of life has thus been hidden from your sight? Up to now, you have not had the divine sense of life. From now on, will you at least know how to read and use events? Is it not deplorable that Christian souls, who should know God and recognise His action, remain in an almost absolute ignorance, and that, precisely by this ignorance, they should render most of His graces useless? In fact, by not recognising them, they do not correspond to them; and by not corresponding to them, they do not use them. Oh, what a terrible disease ignorance is!

V ACTUAL GRACE

But it is good to take a closer look at what actual grace is. You know that God is its Author, you know its tools, which are creatures, you know how it comes to us; that is, with the activity of creatures under the hand of God. But what is it in essence?

As I have already told you, this grace is called actual, because it is produced by a movement, by an action of the creature under the hand of God, and because it communicates activity to you. Properly speaking, actual grace is that divine activity, that supernatural action that you undergo. It is therefore a supernatural impulse that God produces in your faculties, both of Himself and through the creatures that He sets in motion. I say, "both of Himself and through creatures" — in fact, I have shown you the action of creatures under the hand of God and I insist on this specifically — in order to draw your attention to a very practical point about your life, of which you know so little.

But God can also act directly in you, with those intimate touches that saintly souls know so well, and which, undoubtedly, your state of dissipation has prevented you from experiencing so far. I dare not speak to you about these

immediate relations of your soul with your God; He Himself
will show them to you better by letting you taste them, if
you consent to enter into His intimacy. But of what exactly
does this impulse, which is grace, consist? You know that
you are mind, heart and senses. It is therefore your mind,
your heart and your senses that are moved: a movement of
light in the mind, a movement of warmth in the heart, a
movement of force in the senses. This is actual grace: light to
make the mind see; warmth to make the heart love; strength
to make the senses act.

You know that you must know, love and serve God; you
have seen how high you have to climb. Well, it is in view
of this infinite work that grace, carried by the activity of
creatures, comes at every moment to strike your mind, your
heart and your senses. It begins by urging and exciting; then
it sustains, animates and vivifies. It warns you and accompa-
nies you. It begins the divine work without you and carries
it out together with you. In this way, theologians distinguish
between prevenient grace and subsequent grace.

The touches of grace vary infinitely. Your soul's careless-
ness leaves you scarcely suspecting the truth of the influences
that you experience; the encounters that your being has
with the objects around you are too innumerable for you
to grasp their action. In this way, you can see how infinitely
God varies His work in you and how much work there is to
do. Yet, with such great variety, He proposes a single purpose: your improvement as a Christian, the expansion of
your life, the supernatural fulfilment of your being. Nothing
ever fails to do this: everything converges towards this result.

Therefore, God proportions the measure and quality of His graces to the needs of your life, according to the designs of His mercy and to how you correspond to His action. In fact, grace increases or decreases, becomes more or less penetrating, and insinuates itself more or less into your faculties depending on whether you resist it by sin or indulge it by virtue. These influences, exerted on you by the ordinary movement of creatures under the hand of God, constitute what theologians call the ordinary means of grace. No one is refused these ordinary means, since they are everywhere and for everyone.

But God's mercy reserves for itself certain extraordinary blows of grace. When He struck St Paul on the road to Damascus or Pierre de Quériolet in Loudun, when He sent St Catherine of Siena to the pope in Avignon to tell him to return to Rome, or St Joan of Arc to the heart of France to liberate it — in general, every time He acts with a miraculous intervention, this is extraordinary grace.

On the other hand, Our Lord instituted real accumulators of graces in His Church. I refer here to prayer and the sacraments, of which I will speak to you in Part Four. These accumulators have unlimited power, and those who wish to have recourse to them can obtain the most extraordinary and abundant help. You have them in your hands, and they are completely at your disposal. If, by neglecting to make use of them, you are too poor in divine strength and do not have the energy to climb to the heights to which God is calling you, is this not your own fault?

VI ACTUAL GRACE (CONTINUED)

Actual grace is therefore a movement of light in the mind to make it see, of warmth in the heart to make it love, and of strength in the senses to make them act; but to see, love and accomplish what? Now you will see even more clearly how this grace is actual. The light penetrates your mind and makes it see exactly what it needs to see at that moment. The warmth strikes your heart and leads you to love precisely what you must love in that instant. The strength strikes your senses and urges them to do precisely what they have to do at that moment. As you can see, we are dealing with help given at a particular moment.

Once again, you could not imagine how, at every moment, God is proportioning His action to the needs of your life. It is no coincidence that His light strikes your mind, His warmth your heart, His strength your senses. It is no coincidence that this light is projected on the objects that you see, this warmth on the things that you must love, this strength on what you have to do. Actual grace always touches the right point of your faculties, of the purpose of your faculties. It is like a lantern which only reveals exactly that which must be illuminated — which God wants to be illuminated — and leaves the surrounding points in darkness.

If you knew how to conform yourself to this action, you would never be distracted; and the reason is obvious. Since the movement of God makes you see only what you must see, love and do, moment by moment, neither your mind, nor your heart, nor your senses can wander to the right or to the left, towards those diversions which are distractions.

If one follows the movement of God, one does not go right or left, one is never distracted. If now you are continuously distracted, the reason is that you have never been able to conform yourself to the movement of grace, because you have not recognised it.

If only you followed the movement of grace, you would never be restless. Where does this restlessness come from? It comes either from the fact that you don't see what you have to do at a given moment, or from the fact that you worry about the future. When you understand grace, your eye will see in the present moment with the clarity that God wills, and you will have the determination and the strength that you need, since grace gives you light, warmth and strength; and it seems to me that this should be enough for you. You will also understand that we must not think about the future, since the future will bring with it its own grace, which will be enough for it. Do you not know how emphatically Our Lord has recommended us never to be upset? Read chapter six of St Matthew's Gospel, especially the end of the chapter, which I cannot reference here in full.

How easy and simple is the interior life of a Christian who abandons himself to the activity of grace! Listen to an example. You have certainly heard of St John Bosco, that miraculous saint, who did extraordinary works. Well, one day, I wanted to know more deeply about the sanctity of this soul, so I asked one of his religious, who lived closely with him for thirty years in the midst of his countless works, various questions about his interior life. I asked him, among other things, whether Don Bosco was ever worried. — "Don Bosco," he replied to me, "never thought in any one minute, about what he was going to do in the next minute." Here is a saint who understood the action of grace. I quote this fact, to let you see first-hand how the saints act and how far they progress. You too must learn to follow this movement of grace if you want to progress in the Christian life.

VII TEMPTATION

"I understand that the good movements produced in me, by the action of beings who are in the hand of God, can mean just as many actual graces. But not all movements are of this kind. How many bad impressions, dangerous solicitations, dishonest encounters there are! Certainly these are not movements of grace."

We call all these stimulations by the generic name of "temptation". I can tell you that even temptation brings its own grace with it. After all, what is temptation and why is it given to us? Its true providential purpose is to enlighten your mind as to your state, to awaken your heart and to test your strength. "He that hath not been tried, what manner of things doth he know?" (Ecc 34:11). It is the Holy Ghost Who says this. Do you see how temptation is useful to your mind, to teach it an infinity of things about itself and everything else that you would not know otherwise? "Blessed is the man that endureth temptation," says St James, "for when he hath been proved, he shall receive a crown of life, which God hath promised to them that love Him" (Jm 1:12).

Do you see how temptation strengthens love, making it strong and sincere? "My brethren," says the same Apostle, "count it all joy when you shall fall into divers temptations; knowing that the trying of your faith worketh patience. And patience hath a perfect work" (v. 2–4). Do you see how temptation benefits your actions, purifying them and making them perfect? Then you see that, in God's plan, the purpose and result of temptation are the same as those of all other created activity.

No doubt the tool of temptation is often bad in itself, just as its intention is bad; but what does the tool and its intention matter? What matters is God's intention. "And God is faithful, who will not suffer you to be tempted above that which you are able: but will make also with temptation issue, that you may be able to bear it" (1 Cor 10:13). So, even that which seems most contrary to your advancement instead becomes a means, and what seems to be in direct opposition to grace becomes its channel. Once again: everything is a tool in the hands of God; everything, even obstacles.

God sows problems under your feet in a particular order, as is done with problems assigned to anyone learning a trade. The apprentice must be constantly kept in training; once he has overcome one problem, he is presented with another, and by climbing from one problem to the next, he ends up reaching the perfection of his art. Is that not how we learn everything in this world? Is that not how all formation takes place? Divine formation follows no other path; and temptations are nothing other than problems gradually sown under your feet, to force you to climb and to keep yourself exercising. This is how your numbness and weaknesses are shaken off one by one, this is how your strength develops.

If you give up, it is because you are a coward and a bad apprentice. When a man cares about the work, he is not afraid of problems. He rejoices who has a sincere desire to progress, because he tells himself that if the teacher quickly multiplies the problems it is because he judges him capable of making rapid progress. Note that it is up to the teacher gradually to assign the problems, and not the apprentice. In fact if the apprentice, who does not know the trade, wanted to tackle the problems on his own, he would get lost and wear himself out in a useless waste. This means that we must never seek temptation; "he that loveth danger shall perish in it" (Ecc 3:27). But one must be able to face manfully those temptations which God places on his path and overcome them all without blinking. *Sic itur ad astra* — "thus does one journey to the stars". My God, do not allow me to fall into temptation (cf. Mt 6:13). There are two sure ways to fall into it: seeking it out and fearing it. So, cowardice is banished and, with that, you are safe.

VIII YOUR DUTY

Actual grace urges your mind, your heart and your senses to put themselves into action. In this way, God, with His action, demands that you do your part also. What contribution does He ask of you? What does He want you to do?

Oh, very little compared to what He does. He asks you to keep the Commandments of God, the Commandments of the Church, and the duties of your state. Here is your duty, the whole of your duty. This is what you owe to God, and what He demands of you. He requires nothing more than the observance of His Commandments and the practice of your duties of state. You know the Commandments of God and of the Church. But do you also know enough about your duties of state? And do you know the place that they must occupy in your life?

The Commandments of God and of the Church are identical for all men, in all ages, in all places and in all conditions. But does everyone have to observe them in the same way? No, everyone must practise them in the measure proper to their state. On the other hand, he who wishes to be perfect — and you wish to be perfect — must practise certain Evangelical Counsels. What is it that determines for each man how he is to keep the Commandments, and which part of the Counsels he is to follow? It is his duties of state. You see therefore that one's duties of one's state determine two things: 1) the personal way in which the Commandments must be observed; 2) the Evangelical Counsels to be practised.

Indeed, the religious and the layman, the priest and the soldier, the peasant and the magistrate, have the same Commandments to observe, but they do not observe them in the same way. They too must practise the Evangelical Counsels if they wish to be perfect; and yet these Counsels are not the same for everyone. Duties of state dictate to each one what he must do in matters of the Commandments and Counsels. So, if you want to pursue, in a Christian way, whichever career God has destined for you, begin by knowing your duties of state, which will explain to you all your obligations. And, if you want to know where they are to be found, remember that, for the priest, they are contained in ecclesiastical laws, for the religious in his rule, for the layman in the laws proper to his profession. Each state of life has its professional duty, and each professional duty has its own rules that determine it. And it is according to these rules of professional duty that each man must know how to embody, first of all, the Commandments of God and of the Church, and, then, the part of the Evangelical Counsels that apply to his state.

You should never consider the Commandments or Counsels outside this framework; because outside the framework of professions, we expose ourselves to applying them in the wrong way. Do you think that the practices of a Carmelite are suitable for a mother of a family, or those of a Carthusian for a student? Would you call Christian the magistrate whose main care was for his farm, or the father of a family who did not understand nor practise his duty according to the sacred requirements of marriage and fatherhood? Any man who does not know how to see his duty in light of his vocation, who does not practise the Commandments and Counsels according to the needs of his state of life, manifests all the effects of an injured brain or a broken heart.

I am confident at least that there are no fundamental flaws in your understanding or your desire; desiring to be a Christian, you will have the fulfilment of your duty at heart, and to this end, you will apply yourself to seeing and understanding the duties of your state of life.

IX THE FULFILMENT OF DUTY

In short, the whole of your duty is embodied for you, in a concrete and positive way, in your duties of state, so that your work in this world is ultimately summed up in this: knowing, loving and fulfilling the duties of your state of life. Know them, love them and fulfil them, as God imposes them on you and because He imposes them on you. It is here that we must know how to avoid the illusions of self-interest, the fluctuations of caprice, the petty calculations of cowardice, and the false pretexts of passion.

Duty is duty; it imposes itself on you. It is not you who creates it; you have to take it as a whole body. If you mutilate it according to your convenience, you will have nothing more than the remains of a body. Note furthermore that duty is something alive, made up of a soul and a body: the body of duty is the letter of the prescriptions which, in their various articles, make up the law as its members; the soul of duty is the will of God, which inspires, penetrates and animates these prescriptions. According to the expression of St Paul, "the letter [in itself] killeth, but the spirit quickeneth" (2 Cor 3:6).

If you want to live in your duty, you must not kill it: you must take it up alive, in spirit and to the letter, with its soul and body. When you make a choice between the prescriptions that suit you and those that do not, firstly, you no longer have the soul of duty since, by making such a choice, you are following your own will and not that of God; and, secondly, you have only shreds of the body, since you take some parts and leave others. What interior life could there be under such conditions?

If you want to live in your duty, take it up alive — that is, in its entirety — and cling to its soul, that is, to the will of God. Until you see in your duty that great thing, which is its life; until you accept it without calculation, without diminishing or dividing it, you will understand nothing about the matter of duty, and it will be nothing to you but an annoying burden. Nothing is so beautiful and sweet, nothing is so strong and fortifying as living duty; nothing is so hateful and overwhelming as duty dead and picked over.

If duty has cost you so much until now, blame yourself. Why did you kill it? Be once and for all a man of duty, of integral duty, not of your whims and passions; not a man of expedients and compromises, but a man of duty, always; and, just as a bird does not complain about the weight of its wings, neither will you complain any longer about its weight; and you will understand and savour those words of the Saviour: "My yoke is sweet and my burden light" (Mt 11:30).

I cannot indicate to you the distinctive traits of your duties of state; it is not detailed advice that I am giving you here, but the general principles of your life; the guidelines of your conduct. It is enough for me to show you the task and the place of your duties of state in the economy of the work of your perfection, and to show you the substantial way according to which you must put them into practice. It is up to you to add all the particularities. What I am trying to form in you is not the exterior regularity of a more-or-less mechanical life. I do not want to give you a rule, which is not to say that you do not need one; a rule is necessary for man, like the bark of a tree: just as the sap cannot circulate in a tree without the protection of the bark, neither can the current of divine life circulate in the soul without the protection of a rule. But neither the bark nor the rule is itself life.

Rules are found everywhere; they abound, and superabound; there is no need for me to add to those which exist already. But that which is less abundant, that which holds too small a place in most of our assumed arrangements, is the sap; that is, the inner spirit that constitutes life. This is what I would like to form in you. The only good I aim for, the only fruit that this little work is intended to bear for your soul, is the Christian spirit. If only your life could be animated by this breath, filled with this sap, nourished by this substance! O my God! "Thou shalt send forth thy spirit, and they shall be created: and thou shalt renew the face of the earth" (Ps 103: 30).

X DUTY AND PERFECTION

Duty: this is your only job. You have to do only one thing to reach the highest peak of Christian perfection, to consume yourself in the most sublime holiness. God asks only one thing of you, and that is to observe your duties of state. Do you understand? You must never abandon your duties of state, which include the Commandments and Counsels. You see how simple and practical a thing this is. It is by no means a question of doing exceptional things: in fact, that is forbidden; when there are exceptional things in the lives of the saints, it is God Who does them. For your part, you must simply follow the common line of duty, the practical duty of each day, in the condition in which God wants you. All duty and nothing but duty; this is your perfection. This perfection is for all states of life, and is within reach of everyone. Who is there who cannot do his duty? And doing one's duty is all that God asks; He has never asked and will never ask for anything else.

Do not come and tell me — "It is difficult to be a Christian in such and such a condition; perfection is impossible in such and such a state." First of all, let us not overestimate the difficulties; a brave man always overcomes them. Then, consider whether there is a duty to be done in such a state? — "Yes." — Then fulfil the duty of this state and be content with it. When I say "fulfil", I mean, fulfil it as God imposes it and because He imposes it. Is this impossible? Never. It would be blasphemy to say that God imposes impossible duties. So, go all the way with your duty — your duty, not your neighbour's duty — and you will reach the complete perfection that God demands of you.

The cowardice of our bad nature often throws us into a deplorable illusion. One says to oneself, "I would do better in such and such a state of life — it is easier for this man or that man to be a Christian"; one begins to desire another state and does not fulfil the duty of one's own state in the meantime. This is exactly what the enemy of your perfection wants. Be more positive: always stay where you are, and from there, start doing what needs to be done. If, later on, God leads you to a different state, perform the duty of that state also, always living practically the life in which you find yourself. There is nothing so positive as the Christian life; it is not by cradling oneself in empty utopias or wandering around in pious figments of the imagination that Christians are made. Duty; the duty of the moment; pure and simple duty in its concrete reality, whatever it is; herein lies everything.

Be firm and constant in the fulfilment of your duty, and you will be a Christian. Be faithful to the duty of your first vocation, because every vocation has its own duty, and this is what must be done. You necessarily have your own duty — a personal duty — because you necessarily have a vocation.

XI VOCATION

I do not want to ask you if you know your vocation; this is a question to address with your spiritual director, but I want to ask you if you know what a vocation is. Before knowing what your vocation is, you must know what a vocation is. Perhaps you do not have a precise idea.

Tell me, do you think God created you by chance? Certainly not. He knew when, why and how He would create you. And He gave you a set of faculties, attitudes and tendencies corresponding to His idea of you. Do you believe that, after creating you, He threw you into life at the mercy of all eventualities? Not at all. In His counsels, He fixed a place for you and assigned you a role; and it is in view of this role that He gave you all that you are, and continues to direct you every day. The existence that He gave you, the purpose that He set for you, the role that He assigned you, the direction He has in your regard, is everything that makes up your vocation.

I think you understand that, in life, we are not isolated atoms. You know that we are part of the great Body of Christ, which is the Church; you know that we are His members, in this world and in Heaven. A body is made up of very different members, and each member has a place and a function to perform in the body. Observe your body: how many different members and organs, each with its own function! The eye has its function. The hand, the foot, the heart, the veins, the bones, the nerves; everything has its function and its proper place. The diversity of functions produces the complete functioning of the body and its organic integrity. You know this.[9]

Have you observed that no organ has received its function for its own sake, but for the service of the body? What a marvellous thing! The eye, which is made to see, does not see itself, but sees all the other limbs, and, as the servant of all other members, it has this function of seeing. The same is true of all the organs. Each has its own function, and its function is at the service of everything else.

This is a vocation and the reason for this infinite variety among vocations and among souls. Each soul has its own vocation, because each has its function to fulfil: not for itself but for the Body, which is the Church. Thus, he who has the common vocation of marriage does not have it for himself,

[9.] See Part I, Chapter 8.

but for the Church: in order to provide her with children. He who has the vocation of immolation by penance and prayer does not have it for himself but for the Church, which his sacrifice is destined to sanctify.

You are a Christian. Therefore, you are a member of the Church: you belong to her Body. In this Body, you have to occupy a place. Which place? What is your vocation? Whether it is civil, ecclesiastical or religious does not matter much. What matters is that you persevere in your vocation and fulfil its duties. What good is a member which is dislocated? It makes the whole body suffer, and suffer horribly; see what a sore nerve or a dislocated bone produces.

It is therefore necessary for you to stay in your place — the place that your vocation assigns to you — and to fully accomplish the duty of your function in that place; and you do this first for the Church — that is, for God — and then for yourself. So, be a man of your vocation: a man of your duty for God, for the Church and for yourself. Understand and follow your vocation; see that, like all religion, your vocation is not a question of selfishness but of dedication. How great everything is when considered in the true light of faith! You will see how great you are when you see what you are in the eyes of God and the Church! Believe me, your ideas about God and about your soul — about religion and about your vocation — will never be broad enough as long you see them exclusively from the point of view of personal interest.

Down here as well as up there, your vocation calls you to be someone and to do something in the Church of Christ for the glory of God. On earth as in Heaven, seek your vocation in the Body of Christ; and tell yourself that it is, above all, a function to be performed for God and that, precisely by fulfilling this function, you will obtain in full measure the great reward, which is called salvation. Salvation will be granted to you in a very large measure if you know how to observe your vocation with the breadth that I have shown you. "Give, and it shall be given to you: good measure and pressed down and shaken together and running over shall they give into your bosom. For with the same measure that you shall mete withal, it shall be measured to you again" (Lk 6:38).

XII FOLLOW ME

So, here are the general lines of what God does and of what you must do — of God's action on one hand, and yours on the other. Should these two actions be carried out in isolation and independently of each other? Of course not; they must go hand in hand and one must take the other with it. In the formation of your life, God cannot do anything without you and you cannot do anything without Him. If you do not lend it your contribution, His action does not penetrate you; and if His action does not penetrate you, your action is nothing but sterile and useless boredom.

These two actions must go hand in hand. But who is the one who should direct the movement? Is it necessary to ask? When God calls us, He always tells us, "Follow me". Did you happen to see any cases where God said, "Go before me"? Our Lord said to all His disciples, "If any man will come after me, let him deny himself, and take up his cross, and follow me" (Mt 16:24). This is always how He calls us. "Come ye after me" (Mt 4:19). So you have to follow God.

This is how it is done. God, by His action, produces in you the activity that I have tried to make you understand, which is actual grace. If you lend yourself to this movement, He takes possession of you and you, in turn, go into action, and are then supported by the action of grace to see, love and perform the specific duty which falls to you. In this way your action is provoked, supported and measured by that of God. This union is precisely your strength. "I can do all these things in Him who strengtheneth me," says St Paul (Phil 4:13).

Duty in such conditions is made doubly easy for you: first of all, because you do not take on too much or too little of it, since it is God Who measures it; then, because you are not carrying it alone, since God is with you. It is for this reason that Our Lord calls duty a yoke. A yoke always supposes two necks, on which it rests at the same time. What can be hard or difficult about a job that God does with you? I understand very well that when you want to act alone and without care for God's action, you are easily crushed: the task really is too heavy for your shoulders alone. Therefore, we must begin by accepting what God does, and act in accordance with this acceptance. He who blasphemes against God, murmuring against the weather and events, trials and setbacks, sufferings and unpleasant encounters, does not want to know about God's action, does not want to submit, and is in opposition to God; how will he act in a Christian way later? First, he necessarily has to submit.

On the contrary, when you know how to accept things, what beautiful prayers spring from your heart! How your courage comes alive! How the virtues of patience, self-denial, fortitude, generosity, trust and love grow! To a soul that knows how to accept things, God can come and ask for anything — even martyrdom — and it would be capable of this. The soul that murmurs is not capable of anything other than getting upset and collapsing.

When God's action is exercised in you in the form of consolation, you are ready to accept it. You take consolation, but what do you do with it? You sit there enjoying it, and you rest in this enjoyment, and forget your duty because of it. In this way, you do not follow God, Who poured this drop of oil into your soul, to ease it whilst it does its duty, and to give it strength and enthusiasm for the journey. Yet you, disavowing the attention of divine goodness, take this as a pretext to fall asleep in a joyful and selfish laziness. If you respond so badly to the invitations and exhortations of your God, are you surprised that you are not making progress? Understand His action a little better, know how to follow Him with greater sincerity, and you will see how easy it will become for you to progress.

See also how, here, the Christian life is positive and practical. What must be accepted is the situation of the present moment as God arranges it. There is no question of dreaming of other states of life; you have to take the one you are in as it appears, and take advantage of it to do your duty. Tell me if there can be anything more positive. Perhaps it is also because it is so positive that cowards and daydreamers are afraid of it.

XIII THE SCHOOL OF GOD

All arts and all sciences can only be learned, solidly and quickly, from a master. The science of the Christian life is the most sublime of all: it must be learned under the guidance of a Master. Who is the Master? There is only one: "for one is your Master" (Mt 23:8). You have to go to His school and become His disciple; since "it is written in the prophets: And they shall all be taught of God" (John 6:45).

And what is the school of God? You know it now, if I have managed to make you understand the action of grace. God speaks and acts through all creatures. He therefore keeps a school, a practical school, everywhere; to be taught, you need only listen to Him and follow Him. Of course, God's teachings are not deficient, and He teaches each person in a particular way; because what He does for you, He does only for you; He has an action, a teaching, and a special rule of behaviour for you. What is missing are docile disciples. Confess that you have until now been a bad disciple in God's school and that you have listened to Him only a little and understood His lessons very slightly.

What does God teach in His school? He teaches everything, absolutely everything that your vocation requires you to know, love and do. Your vocation requires you to perfect your mind, your heart and your senses, so as to serve God according to all the demands of His glory and of your state. This supposes that you will practise all the Christian virtues proper to your condition. Now it is precisely these virtues, and all of these virtues, that God tries to form in you. In fact, the succession of events, directed by Him and by which your life is divided, leads you to the longed-for opportunity to practise patience and faith, generosity and confidence, self-denial and gentleness, fortitude and prudence, charity and justice, etc.

What virtues, then, must you practise? Those that God teaches you, and for which the opportunity presents itself: do not fear that He will forget some of them; He is a Teacher Who forgets nothing. At what time, and in what order should you practise them? At the moment He presents you with the opportunity, and in the order in which He decides to ask you. That is the right moment and the desired order. God is most skilled in the formation of souls. How Christian you will be if, letting yourself be formed by Him, you practise the virtues of your state at the time and in the order desired by providence!

And what penances will you do? Those that He sows every day on your path. "Sufficient for the day is the evil thereof" (Mt 6:34). Take these penances, those imposed on you and proposed by duty, by events and by the inspirations that come from Him. These are His, and they are better than yours, which, invented on a whim, do not have grace, while His always have it. Yours are often imprudent, dangerous, fallacious, while His never are; yours are inconstant, capricious, incoherent, while His are measured, continued, reasoned; yours often correspond very little and badly to the needs of your growth, while His are always proportionate to you. And in terms of dedication and charity, what will you practise? Whatever God asks of you, and in the circumstances in which He asks you. If you only knew how comfortable it is to let yourself be guided and led by the hand of God! How beautiful, better and more practical!

Is it not regrettable that so many souls, full of lofty Christian aspirations, disown this school of God, and stray in the difficult paths of human turmoil? They have good will, and make great efforts, and end up tired and helpless. Because, in fact, says St Paul, "it is not of him that willeth, nor of him that runneth, but of God that sheweth mercy" (Rom 9:16). So, go to the school of God, and be a true and faithful disciple of the Master. Do you know why so many efforts, so many resolutions, so many rules of life, make for nothing but disastrous results? Because man does such things with his own mind, without following the movement of God. The pupil who does not listen to the teacher will never make progress.

XIV HUMILITY

Do not be surprised if I send you back to school. God's school is great and beautiful. "Blessed is the man whom Thou shalt instruct, O Lord: and shalt teach him out of thy law!" (Ps 93:12). Do not worry, this is not something in which you will acquire the spirit of a student, or else make yourself too small. You know that I have a strong desire for you to be a magnanimous man. You know I want your life to have the fullness of its development. What breadth and righteousness I desire for your mind! What energetic generosity for your heart! What purity for your senses! I will certainly not be the one to repress the impulses of your soul; I do not think that God has given you faculties so as to suffocate them. But neither do I think that He gave you any to waste. I am not afraid of your impulses, but I fear your deviations. Be wary of pride, for in no other thing does human life sink and perish more miserably. "Because every one that exalteth himself, shall be humbled; and he that humbleth himself, shall be exalted" (Lk 14:11). Do you know what pride is? Do you know what humility is? It is very important that you know this.

Pride is your life directed by you and for you. Humility is your life directed by God and for God. So far, by teaching you to glorify God first and God alone, have I not taught you enough how to live for God? To concern your whole life with His glory, and not your pleasure? And this is what humility basically consists in. Because humility does not consist in having nothing, but in attributing everything to God. The more one has received from God, the more one can attribute to Him; and the more one attributes to Him, the humbler one is.

Consequently, the humblest of all is he who, having received the most, attributes everything to his Master. To deny or suffocate in oneself the gifts of God is nothing but lying and laziness. Attribute everything you have, therefore, to Him and you will have a solid foundation of humility. But this is not enough. If you wanted to go to God on your own, with the natural forces of your mind, heart and senses, this would still be pride, and you would not reach Him; rather you would return to yourself. Why? Because, for your part, you cannot escape from yourself. He alone can lift you up to Himself. In fact, your life as a Christian is a supernatural life; and this life is above you, and it is God Who produces it in you, and it is He alone Who can produce it.

In matters of the supernatural life, you are incapable of letting even a simple thought spring forth from the depths of your being (2 Cor 3:5). Remember the fundamental principle stated at the beginning of this book.[10] Life does not exist except by virtue of the interior vital principle. Now the principle of your Christian life is God, Who lives in you and gives life to your thoughts, your affections and your actions.

In terms of natural life, what can your body do without your soul? What thought, what feeling, what act is it capable of without it? It is radically impossible for a corpse to have, of itself, the slightest movement of life. The soul is the life of the body, and the body is only active insofar as the soul vivifies it. United with it, it sees, hears, speaks, acts. Likewise in your life as a Christian, you can do nothing, absolutely nothing, without God (cf. John 15:5). It is He Who produces supernatural life in your soul, in the same way that the soul produces natural life in the body. Would it not be absurd that the body should wish to live without the soul and act on its own? It is equally absurd for a Christian soul to want to live in a Christian way by itself — without God. With Him, and through Him, one can do everything (cf. Phil 4:13); without Him, one can do nothing.

So, you understand and see that you must not have confidence in yourself, nor lean, nor rely on yourself, since you cannot do anything. Whenever you lean on yourself, you are sure to fall. You have already fallen often — perhaps

[10.] See Part I, Chapter 4.

seriously — and always from confidence in yourself. Most likely, you still do not understand this very well; but when you have learned to penetrate a little deeper into the secrets of your soul, you will grasp it much better. And, certainly, if up to now you have shameful experiences of your weakness, should you be surprised? You have wanted to act alone, by yourself, on a whim. And you have found this yoke hard, and its weight considerable? I can well believe it. But why do you turn religion upside down? You always lean and rely on good intentions, on your own efforts, on your rules, your gimmicks; in a word, always on yourself. All these things are good in themselves but, without God, they are only corpses. God alone gives life to all of this. In your religion, you have a manic desire to be first and to act alone; while true religion is God first, God alone. Am I not right in saying that you are doing religion upside down?

If only you knew how to let yourself be led by God, and to bend once and for all to the movement of His grace, then each act of your mind, heart and senses would soon become supernatural; that is to say, Christian. You would live under God's impulse, and then you would truly live for God. And this would be great and true humility in you; you would not keep for yourself any of that which is given to you by God: everything would be referred to Him. What greatness! What a life!

Humility is divine, since it attributes everything to God; pride is pagan, since it refers everything to man. Pride is essentially small, since it lowers you in yourself; humility is infinite, since it lifts you up to God. See how the word of the

Saviour proves true: whoever is full of pride is humbled; and he who humbles himself is exalted. Humility is the virtue of great souls, and pride is the vice of narrow souls. Will you still be afraid of going to the school of the Divine Master? Are you not determined to receive true life from Him, the divine life of your mind, heart and senses? No doubt you want to be His disciple; you want to learn from Him how to live for him.

XV DOCILITY AND VIRILITY

What is necessary for him who wishes to be a humble disciple of the Divine Master? Two things: docility and virility. The docility to accept, the virility to act; flexibility in acceptance, energy in action. We must listen and follow: these are the conditions of humility. First of all, to listen to God's teachings and to accept His orders, then to follow the line of duty and to practise the virtues required. So, docility must go first, and virility must follow. Never in any school is serious progress made in any other way.

Without virility, docility would be nothing more than letting go, and could easily degenerate into cowardice and foolishness. Without docility, manhood would be nothing but pride and would inevitably lead to all sorts of diversions. Combine these two things: be meek and strong; meek before God, and strong — through Him — against yourself. Be pliable under the hand of God, energetic and unyielding against all other actions. Seriously become a practical and practising disciple of the Divine Master. You see that you have to know how to be practical; for such are the lessons of God, and the events by which He leads you. Is there anything else that is so practical and positive? This is what you must understand. And to understand it, you must be practical. But you also need to know how to do it, and that is why you need to practise.

Let us further clarify this with examples. You have friends — undoubtedly you have several — and they are true friends. You also have enemies — and who does not? You have them because God wills it and disposes things so; because, if He did not will them, you would not have them. With your friends, you find consolation and it is very sweet. Desolation comes to you with your enemies, and it is most bitter. Must you hate one and enjoy the other? If you do this then you do not live as a Christian but as a pagan and a tax collector (Mt 5:46–47). To be a Christian, you must make use of the the pains of one and the joys of the other, in order to develop your virtues; since, in reality, pains and joys are nothing other, nor can be anything other, than instruments of virtue. God gives you friends and enemies, just as He gives you successes and setbacks, health and sickness, praise and contradictions, fortune and discomfort; He gives you all things, that is, with a view to your development in the order of your vocation — for His glory.

If the purpose of your life continues to be the pursuit of your pleasure, you will also continue to see in your friends only a source of joy, and in your enemies a source of annoyance; you will continue to enjoy one and detest the other, according to the very petty interest of profit and of your well-being; you will continue to understand nothing about life, to abuse everything and to drift selfishly along. But from the moment in which the glory of God definitively directs your vital movement, both pleasure and contradiction become tools; and you use all that God provides for you to promote His glory and fulfil your duty. And here, I say, is what it means to be a true disciple: a practical and practising disciple of the Divine Master. Be a pupil in His school and you will make progress. "If you continue in my word, you shall be my disciples indeed," says the Saviour (John 8:31).

XVI   THANKS BE TO GOD

Knowing how to accept what God does — the events He arranges, what happens to you every day — convinced that everything comes from His hand, is a science which is sweet to the generous heart, but closed off to the selfish heart. The selfish man, who thinks only of living for himself, will never understand this secret of the Christian life. But the generous-hearted man, who feels the need to give himself, is fully open to it: he tastes its practice by instinct, dives into it boldly, finds in it the best nourishment of his life. He accepts all the dispositions of God without reserve, without hesitation, without curiosity; but above all, he accepts them with love and gratitude.

In gratitude is the unmistakable sign of true souls of God. If you have faith, if your faith makes you see your God in the action that works to your perfection, if you believe that what happens to you is nothing other than the progression of God's incessant work in your soul, if you are convinced that this ongoing work brings you continuous graces, then tell me: what is the feeling that spontaneously emanates from your heart? Is it not gratitude? You say to God, "Thank you!" and you do not know what else to say to Him. And you make no distinction between the things which test you and the things that you like; you know that everything is the teaching of God, the action of God; you know that God is found in consolation and in pain, and you *thank Him* because He comes to you, and because of the work He does in you.

"Thank you, my God!" There is no word dearer to you, no feeling sweeter. "Glory to God!" Thinking of His glory is the purpose of your life. Thinking of the action of God which guides you, you say: "Thanks be to God!" Here are the two simple expressions which, for a Christian heart, express everything. Will they be yours too? Yes, because you are a man who has the ability to taste them! If you did not, then you would not have followed me up to this point. But you must know that these are genuine war cries; they are deployed in a single heartbeat, and hasten to their duty. One gives a sword blow to the enemy, and then keeps going; a touch of spur and the horse charges forward; a trumpet blast to the troops, and they rally. There is no need to repeat these war cries many times, God understands them, and your soul feels them. So, do you see? One of these cries, when let out, especially in suffering, gives the soul a singular strength. It lifts you from the ground, releases the springs of generosity hidden in your heart, awakens the Christian instincts of the soul, and spreads divine strength throughout the whole being.

How joyfully one fulfils one's duty under this impulse! Then we no longer drag ourselves to our duty, we no longer seize up, we no longer hesitate; we rush energetically, happily, for God. "Thanks be to God — glory to God!"

XVII THE WILL OF GOD

Accepting and doing: this is your life. Accepting God's action in order to do your duty is the path of the Christian life. These two elements must complement each other and intertwine to form only one. After all, they are truly one. In fact, both in what you accept and in what you do, there is only one thing which has value and gives life to your acceptance as well as to your action, and that is the will of God. What shall you accept? What God wants. What shall you do? Also what He wants. Accept and do, because He wants it.

In both cases, it is His will which pushes you; which you see, love and follow. Duty would not be duty without the will of God; your acceptance would be meaningless if, in it, you did not seek divine approbation. Here is a comparison that will make you understand better: in a consecrated host, what is it that has value for you? The sacramental species or He Who is hidden under the species? When you communicate, is it the host itself that you are anxious to receive, or Our Lord in the host? Is it not true that the former only has value for you because it contains your God? An unconsecrated host is just a piece of bread, and you do not care about it. A consecrated host, on the other hand, contains your God, and it is Him you adore with the greatest love. You are happy to receive Communion!

Now, the things that we are given to accept and the duty that is ours to perform are true sacraments and true hosts containing the will of God — that is, God Himself, since His will is Himself — and nowhere is He so present to you than where His will is, as I will soon show you. If you do not seek His will in duty and acceptance, these things are absolutely empty for you — as empty as an unconsecrated host — and duty and acceptance have no greater value than would communion with an unconsecrated host. But if you go to your duty to seek God's will there, and if you accept God's will in the provisions of providence, then it is true communion, full union, the mutual embrace of your will with that of God. This is true communion, of which sacramental Communion is itself a means.

In fact, "communion" means "common union" — the common union of man and God. Now, union with God takes place, above all, in the form of a moral union; that is, a union of the will. Union between God and man is accomplished when the will of man unites with that of God. Consequently, when your will meets God's and adheres to it, there is communion. And union between you and God cannot be accomplished in any other way; therefore, you see that God is present to you nowhere else but where His will is: only there can you encounter Him. So, the place of your encounter with Him is duty and acceptance, because His will is there. It is there that His will awaits yours, to unite with it. And, if you see it and embrace it, you really communicate because you enter into union with God. But if you do not see it, you are like an infidel in the presence of the Most Blessed Sacrament. An infidel does not know at all Who is in the sacred host, which for him is a thing without meaning. And the same is true of duty and of all the events of life for the blind Christian who does not know how to worship the will of God in them. Go to the school of God to seek God's will, and you will be in communion with God.

XVIII TRUE COMMUNION

If, through an impossible privilege, the pope granted you permission always to carry with you a ciborium full of hosts and to receive Communion as many times as you wanted, your life would be one continuous rapture. Now, that which the pope will never grant you, God grants you. You always have God's will with you, in everything you must accept and do. Accept and do God's will, and each time this is a new communion. And, in a certain way, it is better than a sacramental Communion, since it is an effective communion, an essential communion of your will with that of God.

I have told you that you receive sacramental Communion solely as a means of bringing about this effective union of your will with that of God. In fact, why do you communicate and receive Jesus? To increase His love in you. And what is His love if not the union of your will with His? Your communion would be sterile if it did not produce love. Full, effective and true communion is therefore the union of your will with that of God. Oh, how many beautiful things does faith reveal — when one has it! However, one must agree that enlightened and living faith is not a common thing, especially today!

But observe the consequences also. If your faith is not yet alive enough to make you see the will of God in the sacrament of things to be accepted and done, it is none-theless illuminated enough to let you know that Our Lord is wholly present in each host and in every part of the host; as wholly in a small one as in a large one, in a fragment as in a whole host. The difference in size and accidents of the host in no way changes the real presence of Jesus Christ. You communicate as much with a small host as with a large one, with a half as much as with a whole, and you see that the priest collects with the same respect and equal veneration even the smallest consecrated particles.

Well, the same is true of God's will. It is always whole, always the same; to be done and accepted in all things, small and large. So why do you despise the little things? Is God's will less valuable because it gives you a little thing to do or to endure? Is God not God equally and everywhere? If you despise Him in little things, is this any way to attest to your faith? Why do you make such a distinction, if not because it is not His will that you seek after all but your own whim? If you want to be a Christian, do not make so many distinctions. If you want to communicate with the will of God, then it is present as entirely in small things as it is in great things, in unpleasant circumstances as much as in those that give you consolation. If you despise it, it is because you have no faith; if you ignore it, it is because you are blind; if you neglect it, it is because you are a coward; if you trample it underfoot, it is because you are a villain.

If you knew how to communicate — that is, to unite your will with that of God — it would not take you long to become a Christian, since this communion can be had at all instants and in all things. If only you knew! Come then, say resolutely with the Saviour that, from now on, your great and substantial food will be to do the will of Him Who sent you into this world, until the perfect fulfilment of the work for which He created you (John 4:34).

XIX IMPERTURBABILITY

If you have the knowledge of this adorable mystery of the divine will hidden everywhere, if you know the secret of this communion, which I have tried to teach you, then misfortune cannot exist for you. Indeed, what really is everything that the world calls adversity and misfortune, and what is that which it calls luck and happiness? It is only a rind, a surface, an appearance; it is the exterior of life. Hidden underneath is a substance, which is the interior: the marrow of life; that is, God's will. Doing God's will is the whole food of the soul; nothing feeds it except this. But how beneficial this food is to it! By uniting with the will of God, the soul expands, its life develops, all its faculties rise to the point of being able to glorify God. You are now serious and want to live at any cost. To live: to grow, to expand, to reach the goal for which you were created — this is the only good which attracts you, because it is in fact your only good; the expansion of your being for the glory of God. Now this enchanting Christian greatness confers everything on you — often pain, and pain more often than joy.

God's will is everywhere. That is why you are always happy wherever you find God working on your growth through His creatures. What does a little pleasure or a little suffering matter to you? This is trifling nonsense for a heart that wishes to live! And look what peace is in this heart! A peace which nothing disturbs, nothing alters and nothing interrupts. A peace which is always the same, calm in joy, calmer still in pain. A peace which welcomes all events and all duties with the same serenity, because everything brings it the same nourishment and the same profit. Christian peace! An absolute imperturbability! Here is the real state of the true Christian. After the glory of God there is nothing so great as the peace of man: thus sang the angels at the manger of Bethlehem (Lk 2:14). Oh, how good it is to be a Christian! Nothing is more valuable than this peace, and I want you to enjoy this equanimity of soul. The man who sets his own pleasure as his life's purpose, who sees the reason for his existence in the happiness he can enjoy, and who is incessantly occupied with the attainment of this happiness through creatures — this man, I say, is continually unhappy, because that which he thinks is the main goal of his life always eludes him.

You still know very little about the evils of this life, and I wish you never to know them. You have just seen how imperturbability is attained in the individual human life. Do you want to see now how it is attained in social life?

"There are no foolish professions, only foolish people," as the old saying goes. What depths of Christian and common sense this proverb embodies! In fact, any profession, any social condition — since it is willed by God for the general good — contains His entire will. The condition of a head of state does not contain it more fully than does that of a street sweeper. God wants different social conditions for the different needs of society; but, varied as these conditions may be, all, without distinction, contain one identical substance, which gives them their value; this is the will of God. Whatever rung of the social ladder we may be on, the only essential thing is to fulfil the divine will.

The world, with its fallacious vanity, can only appreciate the outward appearance of social distinctions; it pities or despises those at the bottom of the social ladder and envies those at the top. The Christian, who knows that the will of the Lord is found on a higher level no more than on one below, considers the man who is below to be just as rich and privileged as the man who is at the top. He does not esteem, he does not envy; he aspires to the sole thing which has a value for him, the will of his God, and he knows that he has it as much below as above. Do you think that a St Benedict Joseph Labre, who sanctified himself by begging, did not have a situation as privileged as that of the popes during whose reign he was begging, and who (unlike him) have not been canonised?

The divine, true and profound equality of souls is thus manifest in the widest array of social functions. No one can complain that God has been stingy with him, for He has assigned His will to everyone, to lead them all to His glory in this way. So, it is profoundly true that there is no foolish profession. But, dear me, how many foolish people there are! How many people whose foolishness appreciates only the exterior of things and feeds only on appearances! Whatever your profession is, therefore, remember that it will never be silly; and make sure that you never become silly yourself. You have the means.

XX SANCTIFYING GRACE

Every time you communicate effectively (that is, every time you unite your will with that of God) sanctifying grace is produced as an outpouring of God in you. St Thomas, therefore, defines sanctifying grace as an influence of divine goodness in the soul, which becomes similar and pleasing to God through this communication, and worthy of eternal life. It is this grace that makes holiness, and therefore it is called "sanctifying".

There is always a preparation, a necessary adaptation, so that this grace can be infused into the soul. In fact, as long as the soul is far from God, the influence of grace cannot be produced. Therefore, it must be close to God, so that He can effuse Himself in it. Thus, for Baptism, the child is brought to the Church and placed under her care. The adult approaches the Church himself, under the influence of that actual grace which I have tried to make you understand. As soon as the soul is close to Him, God effuses Himself in her, communicates Himself to her, and this mysterious infusion of sanctifying grace makes the soul live in God, and God in her.

As soon as the soul is close to God, He effuses Himself in it, communicates Himself to it; and this mysterious infusion of sanctifying grace makes the soul live in God, and God in the soul.

This first union is completely gratuitous; you cannot deserve it in any way. You can and must be willing to receive it, certainly not by your own strength, since actual grace has already been given to you for this, but you must collaborate with grace. When you are ready, God enters into you through a pure act of His goodness, and takes possession of your soul. He is in you and you are in Him, He is yours and you are His, He lives in you and you live in Him. This is the Christian life.

When God lives in you in this way, every time your will encounters His (that is, every time you make an act of conformity to His will) a new rapport takes shape and, in this rapport, a new effusion. In this way, grace increases; God penetrates your soul and takes possession of it in order to transform and infuse it with the supernatural and divine. This is how Christians and saints are made.

You have already understood that every detail of God's action brings an actual grace; now you see that every encounter of your will with God's produces an increase of sanctifying grace; see, then, how many graces there are! What are you still lacking, since the action of God with actual grace is everywhere, and you can encounter God's will everywhere, and find sanctifying grace in union with Him?

Think of the quantity of movements produced in your faculties by everything that touches you internally and externally ... and in all this activity there are actual graces; why do you not take advantage of them? Think of the facility that you have in uniting your will to that of God, which you find everywhere, in your duty and in all things that must be accepted; why do you not participate in this union? If you do not become a Christian and a saint, the fault is a hundred times yours.

The excitement of actual grace is already a movement of life; this impulse that brings light to the mind, warmth to the heart and strength to powers also helps you, in a singular way, to do what you have to do. But when grace — which is true life, the life of God — spreads in your soul and makes it live, it also spreads in the mind, heart and senses; and wherever it goes, it brings divine life, it permeates your soul, until your faculties are, without any deviation, entirely united with God. This is the pinnacle of perfection. What glory you give Him then! Your being is entirely consecrated, given, dedicated to Him; you live in Him and you live for Him. What happiness for you! You enjoy God, and truly "taste, and see that the Lord is sweet" (Ps 33:9).

XXI THE THREE FULLNESSES OF GRACE

But what is this influence of divine goodness in itself, by which God unites you to Himself and makes you live His life? This is the greatest of God's mysteries, since grace is the greatest of the things He has created. It is also a tool of God, because it was created by God. It is the greatest and the first thing that was created. "Wisdom hath been created before all things," says Sacred Scripture (Ecc 1:4). What Scripture calls "created wisdom" is grace in its complete generality, in its universal fullness. God possessed this wisdom from the very beginning of His ways, even before creating anything else (Proverbs 8:22).

Why was grace the first thing to be created? Remember God's plan. The purpose of creation is the union of souls with God, for His glory and for their happiness. The means which brings about this union is grace — actual grace, which prepares it, and sanctifying grace, which establishes it. All other creatures are the vehicles of grace. It was therefore necessary for the great means of union to exist before man, who was made to be united with God; before creatures, who were supposed to be the tools of grace. Grace, therefore, was created first. And to the extent that God made and continues to make other beings, it expands in them. Similar to magnetic influence, it insinuates itself, so to speak, into the creatures destined to be its tools, so that all the activity of created beings can converge in the formation of Christian souls.

Do you know what the greatest masterpiece of grace is? It is Jesus Christ. In Him there is the most perfect union of man with God, since Jesus Christ is the Son of God made man. In Him, human nature is so united to divine nature that there is only one Person. And what is it that made such a union? Grace. It is grace that united the humanity of the Saviour to the divinity of the Word.

What a grace! It alone surpassed all other graces put together. Thus, Jesus Christ has in Himself and for Himself a primitive fullness of grace, which can, in some way, be called infinite; the grace which brought about the mystery of the Incarnation.

After this first fullness, which belongs to the Son of God, there is another that comes close, and it is the one which made the Mother of God. This too is incomparable fullness! After the miracle of the Son of God made man, the greatest prodigy is the Virgin made Mother of God. And to accomplish this miracle, a fullness of grace was needed which was not too far from the first fullness. It is this fullness that you salute, with the Angel, when you say, "Hail Mary, full of grace".

Finally, there is still a third, and it is the one destined to make the children of God. The angels and saints are called to form one Body, all together, which is called the Church. And to form this Body, there is a fullness of grace, which is the fullness proper to the Church. Every member of the Body of the Church — that is to say, every angel and every one of the elect — draws from this fullness that part of grace that is necessary for him, in order to occupy that place in the Body which is intended for him. It is in this third fullness that you take part, and from which you receive the grace that makes you a Christian.

So, here are the three fullnesses of grace: the one belonging to Christ, the other to His Mother, the third to the Church; the first made the Man-God, the second made the Mother of God, the third made the Church of God. Of these three fullnesses, the second is greater than the third, and the first is greater than the other two combined.

By Himself and for Himself alone, Jesus Christ possesses a fullness of incomprehensible and incommunicable grace. But, at the same time, He possesses the fullness proper to Mary and the fullness proper to the Church. In fact, He merited for His Mother the signal grace that she received from Him, and earned all the graces that He communicates to His Church. Actual grace and sanctifying grace: everything comes from Him. Therefore, He alone has, by Himself, the absolute and universal fullness of grace. He is "the Holy One of God" *par excellence* (Mk 1:24). He is holiness personified, and the holy Being Who bears the name of the "Son of God" (Lk 1:35). It is to Him that you must have recourse as the source of all life, if you want to live in a Christian way. How many treasures He has in store for you! It is He, it is the merits of His Passion which spread actual grace through the creatures which are its channels. Through Him and through His merits, sanctifying grace is infused in your soul and in all souls.

So love Jesus Christ, study Him, follow Him. He will make you a Christian. "Let us go therefore with confidence to the throne of grace: that we may obtain mercy, and find grace in seasonable aid" (Heb 4:16).

XXII MARY FULL OF GRACE

Mary is full of grace. And this fullness is the true reason for her greatness. How can I make you understand something of this fullness and this greatness? The Blessed Virgin has a grace which is hers, which is hers alone and which makes her Mother of God. And this unique and singular grace is so great that, by itself, it surpasses all the graces granted to the angels and to the saints. Add up, if you can ... but you will never be able to ... add up at least as many as you can of the infinite number of actual graces distributed throughout the centuries, the immense profusion of sanctifying grace in the angels and saints. As I have told you, all the graces communicated in past centuries and all those that will be communicated in future centuries, all together, constitute the fullness of the Church.

Now, the grace given to Mary to make her the Mother of God alone is greater than all of this. Consequently, Mary alone is a greater miracle of holiness than all the angels and saints put together. After her Divine Son, she is the most perfect of God's works. What greatness! For this, the saints and the doctors have competed in praising her, and they have said wonderful things of her. They never stop singing praises, offering felicitations, and expending themselves in acclaiming her honour. And what have they been able to say? Nothing that is worthy of her, since all the tongues of angels and men put together will never speak adequately of such greatness, which is above them all. If I speak with the tongues of men, and of angels then I still not have said anything about her.

You see how, due to this elevation, Mary is Queen of angels and of men. But this is only her second fullness; she is also Queen by yet another dignity, more immediate in a certain sense, and more effective. In fact, Mary possesses all the fullness of grace which is proper to the Church; and this in order to communicate it. Mary possesses all the graces received by the angels and saints; she has dominion over them, and the entire Church of angels and saints receives them from her.

Mary is the Mediatrix of all Graces. There is no grace which does not come from her heart, and which does not pass through her hands. You and I, like all the sanctified of all times, receive everything from her. Do you therefore understand how she is, in a practical and living way, Queen of Heaven and earth? Finally, all the activity of Heaven and earth is accomplished solely to communicate grace; therefore, they obey the Blessed Virgin, who is the Mediatrix of all Graces. True Queen and Lady, whose will is obeyed by everything in order to distribute to angels and to men the graces of which she is Mistress and Mediatrix! On account of this second fullness, Mary would already be greater than all the angels and saints, since she not only possesses what they receive, but she distributes as Queen and Lady what they receive as servants.

What would it be like then if, to this fullness that she is charged with distributing, you add that which she has for herself and which is incomparably greater? Tell me, do you find your Mother great enough; worthy enough of your praise, your respect, your love and your confidence? I have told you of her greatness (her second fullness) but shall I tell you of her goodness? Consider that she has her greatness in order to communicate it: this second fullness makes her Mother of men; the first makes her the Mother of God.

She is Mother; what more do you want me to say? Come and greet her as Mother of your God and your Mother. Greet her in that incomparable fullness that makes her Mother of God; love to repeat to her the Angelic Salutation which you will now find more beautiful: "Hail, Mary, full of grace". Greet her in that double fullness which makes her Mother of God and men, and say to her that invocation which the Church addresses to her: "Holy Mary, Mother of God, pray for us!"

I will not add anything else. Before the greatness of Mary, I feel the need to contemplate in silence. What could I say that is worthy of her and you? You too need to prostrate yourself in the silence of meditation, and you will find no words in which to express your veneration. Mary, Mother of God, is so great! Mary your Mother is so sweet and good! I will now leave you to venerate her and pray to her; I will leave you to venerate her greatness, pray to her goodness; I will leave you to venerate her in that fullness of grace for which she is the Mother of God; I will leave you to pray to her, because of that fullness by which she is your Mother. Praise her, congratulate her for that incomparable grace which made her the Mother of God; for which you will never praise her enough. Pray to her, invoke her, obtain from her the graces that she has for you. You can never call upon her enough.

Praise of Mary, prayer to Mary: these must be your two incessant acts of love for her. She is the Mother of your God: how can one not praise her? She is your Mother: how can one not pray to her? And these two sentiments of praise and invocation are so well expressed in that prayer, which is the most beautiful after the *Pater* — the prayer you already love so much, but which you will come to love even more — "Hail, Mary": this is the praise; "Holy Mary, Mother of God, pray for us": this is the invocation. Oh, how you will be able to recite the Hail Mary!

PART IV

EXERCISES OF PIETY

I REMEDIES

Why do you take so little advantage of God's countless graces? Because you are sick. Your mind is sick and cannot see; your heart is sick and does not know how to love; your senses are sick and do not know how to act. Therefore, we must heal them, and to heal them we need remedies. What are these remedies? There are some that God Himself has prepared, and others prepared by the Church. They are called, by the generic term, "exercises of piety". What are these exercises of piety? They are not piety itself, but the remedies of piety — piety which does not consist in performing many pious exercises, but in performing them properly — just as health, for a sick person, does not consist in taking an excessive quantity of medicines, but in taking those that are needed. They are remedies, remedies for your spiritual infirmities; they must be used as much as your interior infirmities require, and no more. When a man sincerely wishes to get well, he does not pay much attention to whether the remedy is agreeable or repulsive; he takes it. It is not a matter of whim, but a matter of healing.

Do you see in what a serious, sober and generous way one must know how to understand, love and perform exercises of piety? It is a matter of life or death for you; when one is sick (and, indeed, very sick) one must not mess around with remedies; one has to take them at the proper time and under the necessary conditions, at one's own peril. You know how sick you are in your poor soul! And how much it needs medicine! And how weak you are! Be serious, and learn to heal your soul at least as well as your body. You are resolved to take the remedies that are needed — that is, to perform the exercises of piety which are necessary for you; you are resolved to do this at all costs because, first of all, you want to live as a Christian and not lead the evil-smelling life of those corpses who are called sinners. You do not want to be one of the number of those to whom Jesus Christ said: "whited sepulchres, which outwardly appear to men beautiful, but within are full of dead men's bones, and of all filthiness" (Mt 23:27).

You do not love rottenness of the soul any more than of the body, because you know that rottenness of the soul is more horrible than that of the body, and you esteem your soul more than your body. No rottenness; "God hath not called us unto uncleanness, but unto sanctification" (1 Thes 4:7). Medicines, therefore: remedies to heal, remedies to keep you well.

II THE REMEDIES OF GOD

The first and most important remedies are those that God Himself has prepared for you. Since Our Lord Himself has deigned to prepare certain remedies for your infirmities, and to show you the need and the way of taking them, you must not have the audacity to neglect them. God undoubtedly knows your infirmities, and the means to heal them. Jesus Christ, the Heavenly Doctor sent by His Father to heal the evils of souls, has prepared remedies; He has even prepared them with His Flesh and His Blood. It must be admitted that it would be difficult for a doctor to further press his love for his sick (cf. John 13:1). So, what about the patient who does not want remedies?

The remedies of God are the sacraments and prayer. First of all, you know the sacraments — great treasures of the Church, great remedies of the Christian life. Baptism, which creates this life, Confirmation which strengthens it, Penance which repairs it, the Eucharist which nourishes it, Extreme Unction which crowns it, Holy Orders which perpetuate its ministers, and Marriage which perpetuates individuals: here is the great arsenal of graces, the accumulators of divine strength. Here, Our Lord has concentrated the richest fruits of the Passion.

Is there any need to urge you to use them? Oh no, certainly not! I am convinced that you feel a real need for the two sacraments which are the daily repair and nourishment of your life. If you do not feel the need for (and love of) Confession and Communion, do not tell me that you have the desire to live. If you have to be compelled to approach the holy tribunal and the sacred table, then you lean much more towards your passions than towards God and there is more of a sense of the world than of Christ in you; you reserve for God only a small place and you will, no doubt, come to make it even smaller. You know that "God is not mocked" (Gal 6:7); He must be treated as God; you are convinced of this, and are determined to treat Him in this way.

If you are resolved to be frank with yourself and with God, if you are determined to become a man of faith and duty, then I do not need to tell you when or how you should have recourse to the sacraments. The needs of your soul will inform you sufficiently of this and, until they do, whatever books or men tell you will not have a great influence on you.

The upright heart does not need many sermons or exhortations; what it feels has more value than whatever is said to it. Moreover, by the grace of God, there is so much insistence today on receiving Communion that you are able to hear innumerable admonishments and exhortations. So, I do not have to add my recommendations to the many others, and will only repeat my advice: be sincere, go to the depths of your faith. Do you see? Faith, like love, is not a question of words or language, but is, first of all, a question of truth and action (cf. 1 John 3:18). If only I could convince you of this! If I could teach you to be a man of faith! A man of truth and sincerity! What? Would a Christian, who seriously wishes to live as a Christian, need to be incessantly urged on by exhortations or compelled by surveillance, without which he would fall into inactivity? He would have nothing in his mind or in his heart.

Life does not come from the outside but from within; and, if there is nothing inside, there will never be life. Do not talk to me about those beings without character, who have no more life than a cart; who move when pulled and, as soon as they are put down, stay where they are. You will never belong to the category of those feeble, empty, cowardly, false beings, who do good out of fear or complacency, out of flattery or hypocrisy, out of vanity or self-interest.

Goodness, in order to be true, must be sincere; and if there is one good deed that requires sincerity, it is the frequenting of the sacraments. I shudder at the mere thought of the sacrileges committed by hypocrisy. But I also suffer thinking about the cowardice of hearts that let themselves be dragged away. Oh no, you will never be an empty heart or a false spirit.

III PRAYER

God grants everything to prayer; everything, even miracles. But why does He make us pray? To force us to draw close to Him. Prayer is one of the greatest means of approaching God. If He had placed everything at your disposal without requiring you to have recourse to Him, then you would live at a perpetual distance from Him — using and abusing everything, no longer caring about Him. Look and see if things do not always happen this way. When you do not need anything, God is thought of very little, but being in need leads you back to Him.

Since union with God is the supreme purpose of your life, prayer is your supreme duty. It puts your mind, heart, and senses in relation to Him. It is prayer which gradually stops the habitual distraction of your life. "Distraction", you know, means separation. You live habitually separated from God; your mind, your heart and your senses are busy with things far from Him. This is distraction; it is a great evil, the extent of which you have recognised, and which must be healed. Prayer brings your mind, heart and senses back to God; it restores them to Him, at least for a moment; it accustoms them to living close to Him once again; and, gradually, as prayer becomes more alive and frequent, you live more habitually in union with God. Do you understand why God makes you pray, and why He makes you pray so much? The more He makes you pray, the more you are forced to draw near to Him. There are graces that God does not grant except to prayers repeated and multiplied at length; and the greatest grace is to pray consistently, because, in this way, it assures a more complete coming together with Him.

How happy you will be when you understand this, the reason for prayer! Happier still if you acquire the spirit of prayer — that is, the need to return and to have continual recourse to God, the need to remain in intimacy with Him, the need to speak to Him and to hear Him speak to you, the need to be with Him. I would recommend prayer to all. But to you, who wish to be a Christian in spirit and in truth, who wish to live for God at any cost, you should have the spirit of prayer. A heart which finds prayer burdensome has only a seed of Christian life. Is it possible for someone with good lungs to find breathing difficult? Prayer is the breath of the Christian soul who needs to breathe out towards God and to breathe in the air of God. Prayer must become for your soul as easy, as necessary and beneficial as breath is to your body.

As you can see, prayer, in its essence, is not a formulary. It is a movement of the soul and not a movement of the lips. Undoubtedly, there are formulas that best embody this deep and true movement of the soul towards God, and these formulas help prayer a lot: I will soon tell you which ones are the best. But, in essence, prayer — the spirit of prayer — is the impulse towards and return to God, it is receiving God and life with God. And it is in this sense that Our Lord said that prayer must always continue and never cease (Lk 18:1). Can your body stop breathing? Then why does your soul stop praying? Ceasing to pray is, for the soul, what ceasing to breathe is for the body: suffocation and death.

When your soul prays instinctively, just as your body breathes, then you will be a Christian; it will be a true sign that you are alive. The body which no longer breathes is a corpse; the same is true of the soul. The body which breathes with difficulty is sick; the same is true of the soul. The body which has expansive breath has a strong life; the same is true of the soul. But how can we give the soul this divine power of breathing, which is the spirit of prayer?

First of all, you will manage this under the inspiration and direction of the Holy Ghost, Who comes to the rescue of your weakness. You do not know what you have to ask God for, to pray properly. But the divine Spirit comes to you to form ineffable groans, which are true prayer. And He Who penetrates the depths of hearts also understands the desires inspired by His Spirit, Who forms in the saints a prayer according to God.

In what way does the Holy Ghost form prayer in the hearts of the saints? With all the particularities of divine action which bring grace, which I have previously talked about at length. Therefore, be subject to this action of the Spirit of God, and you will become not only a man of prayer in the ordinary sense of the word, but a man of contemplation. You can also find effective aids in the practices established by the Church.

IV THE REMEDIES OF THE CHURCH

There exists in the Church a considerable quantity of practices and pious formulas introduced by the saints, and approved by her; it is a pharmacy, rich in all types of medicine. There are no diseases in souls which cannot find fitting remedies there. Does this mean that it is necessary to overload oneself with these practices? Tell me, when you go to a pharmacy, do you buy all the medicines that are there? No, you get only the ones you need. Do the same here.

For the soul, as well as for the body, it is first of all necessary to look for a real pharmacist and to be wary of charlatans, who are not uncommon nowadays. The Church is the only pharmacy authorised by God to distribute true medicines to souls. Be relentless therefore in keeping away from all the fictional inventions of unapproved devotions, just as you would from quack remedies. You understand that this is an important recommendation.

Now, in the pharmacy of the good Lord, choose the remedies that are suitable for your soul. — "Which ones?" you ask me. Well, there are the obligatory exercises: Mass on holy days of obligation, those indispensable acts that every Christian must undertake from time to time — that is, acts of faith, hope and charity, annual Confession, receiving Communion during Eastertide, etc. There should be no hesitation in this, because your spiritual health absolutely depends on them. They are remedies that the life of a Christian cannot do without, on pain of death.

Other exercises are matters of counsel, such as morning and evening prayers, Sunday Vespers, attending Mass on days which are not obligatory, regular reception of the sacraments, devotion to Our Lord, to the Blessed Virgin and to the saints, meditation, examination of conscience, etc. To make decisions and determine the right amount here, you need your doctor's advice. Do you know who the doctor of your soul is? He is the spiritual director whom you must consult, because it is up to him to tell you what suits your present needs. Above all, he must be consulted on the third category of remedies — that is, on those that are purely optional. You will hear an infinite number of recommended practices and devotions — drawn only from those that are approved of course; I have already told you what the others are worth, and I will not mention them further.

Beware of two excesses on this point. Firstly, that of denigrating these devotions in themselves; they are good, since they are approved by the Church. If you want to make fun of abuses, you may — I like to lambast all the nonsense which causes religion to be ridiculed — but you have to do it in such a way as to ridicule the abuse, whilst standing up for true devotion. The second excess from which you must protect yourself consists in that abuse which I authorise you to lambast, and includes childishly overloading yourself with an infinity of little things.

Few and good: this is the first rule concerning optional devotions. And here is the second: absolute freedom. You are not obliged to attach yourself to anything and you should feel free to take up these exercises according to the needs of your soul. You must only use them to raise your spirits, your heart and your senses to God. So, they must vary according to whether you are further from or closer to God.

Do you see? Everything must be subordinated to the real needs of your Christian life. No overloading or troublesome obligations; but, at the same time, no disgust or cowardice. Overloading would indicate your ignorance, and cowardice your unwillingness, and these are two very serious symptoms, since not knowing and not willing are the two great diseases of the soul. Try to have neither one nor the other. You must form the spirit of prayer in yourself, expand the breathing of your soul. Have the energy to take the necessary remedies, and the wisdom not to take up any which are useless. Furthermore, be prudent enough not to take up any which are harmful.

In short, what must dominate, guide and excite you in everything is the need for life: you are made to live. And you know what it means to live; I was careful to tell you from the beginning. If you are anxious to live — that is, to develop everything that needs to be developed in you — you must know how to take the medicine and avoid the poison.

Blessed is he who has the instinct for life! And it is precisely this instinct that I am trying to form and awaken in you. You see that I am in no way trying to suffocate you in external regularity; I do not like mummies, no matter how rich the bandages in which they are wrapped. What I love is life; what I seek is for you to live; what I tire myself out for is to make you understand life. You see, a living plant knows how to discern for itself the juices favourable to its nutrition. Have life, and you will know how to choose the remedies useful for your divine growth.

V LOOKING BACK

Let us recall, in a brief summary, the exposition of the Christian life in its essence. First, its purpose is fundamental. The purpose is to get to know, love and serve God first (as we saw in Part One); then God alone (as we saw in Part Two). Then you must work to achieve this purpose by accepting God's action and doing your duty (and that is what we saw in Part Three). Because of the corruption of our nature by sin, our mind, heart and senses are very far from this purpose and from this work. Therefore, it is necessary to place the purpose and the work before your eyes again, in your heart and in your hands. And this is the task of exercises of piety, which we are examining in this fourth part.

Please, hold on assiduously to this fundamental concept of religion, which will be a light and a strength to you. You will see later how many silly things and trivial matters, dark things and inconsistencies, uncertainties and falsehoods it will free you from. Many souls drift through trivial matters because they do not have correct ideas. And I especially do not want you to be a slave to trivial matters. Such a man has a very poor knowledge of what he is, where he is going and what he does. He amuses himself, he wastes his time, he wastes his life. Nothing about him is organised. You will see him attach great importance to certain childish things and neglect the essential points; he will practise many worthless devotions but will not know even his most basic duties. Nothing is so sad as to see such bewildered lives as his. He is like a traveller who takes the first train that comes along, without knowing where he is going. He stops in an unknown place; in this way he starts out on an adventure without having decided where he wants to go, nor the path he must follow, nor the train he must take.

I beg you, do not be an adventuring Christian! In order not to be one, know exactly what your goal is, what your path is and what your means are. And do not confuse these three orders of things. The means are meant only for the path, and the path is meant for the goal. Your exercises of piety are performed in order to make you follow God's will, and you must follow God's will to reach God's glory. This is how you must understand your life if you want to be a serious Christian.

VI   CHRISTIAN PRACTICES

Having recalled this, you should know that the practices introduced by the Church are linked to three fundamental points. Some have the mind for their main object, others concern the heart, and a third type acts more particularly on the senses. It is for the senses, above all, that the Church has the ceremonies of her worship, the solemnity of her feasts, the attraction of her devotions. Are so many means of influencing our imagination intended only to gratify our sensibilities? Of course not. They are rather intended to tear our senses from the attraction of created pleasure and call them back to the service of God. For this reason, the Church does not like noisy displays or performances which imitate the theatre. Alas, things like this are seen too often in certain churches. Flee them.

Christian worship is always serious in its beauty; the splendour of its appearance reflects the serenity of its purpose. This is precisely what you must love. My God, what puppets are those Christians who go to church for the spectacle of vestments, for the trappings of music, decor and oration! As long as you feel that your soul obeys sentiments only of this kind, I have no faith in your Christianity. Look for that which can elevate your senses to God, and not that which makes you rest in the excitement of your eyes and ears. Leave vanity to those enslaved by vanity! What great resources for the heart are found in the exhortations of the Church, in the edifying examples of her heroes, in Christian associations, in works of zeal and charity! The Church would like to have men of character and energy, men with great and strong hearts, men capable of all sacrifices and heroism. How many things have been created to appeal to generous hearts, to make them magnanimous!

Of the saints, which one do you want to imitate? Among the exhortations of the Church, which one will win you over? To which works of zeal for the good of others will you consecrate your life? It is not for me to tell you. This is the great question of your vocation. The Spirit of God,

Who breathes where He wills, will no doubt breathe into your heart, since your heart is open to the breath of God and prepared to dedicate itself generously. I have only one piece of advice for you. Be careful not to follow anything other than the Spirit of God; and, deciding to give your heart away, give it only to God.

Be wary of human exploitation; you will also meet this on the path of good. Today, in the practice of good works, the good will of many is very badly used, and consequently is very sterile. How I wish that your heart would attach itself only to God with that enlightened sincerity which I have strongly recommended to you already. I long for your life to be seriously directed — for the treasures of your heart to be usefully employed — so that nothing which God has given you might be lost; in order to be a man and a Christian, useful to yourself and to others. Let me tell you again everything I wish for you: I long for you to live. "I am come," says the Founder of Christianity, "that they may have life, and may have it more abundantly" (John 10:10). I would like you to be able to taste these words of the Saviour.

Finally, the Church has all manner of instruction for the spirit: its meditations, its readings, its spiritual exercises. There is no shortage of books or words. But, alas, in the books and words of our superficial century, it is often substance that is missing. By the way, allow me to give you some advice regarding your reading: get your mind used to serious books, and never allow it to settle for impressive phrases or flashy style. I have already told you many times that you should not be satisfied with words. Be persistent in keeping your library, like your mind, closed to frivolities. God knows if such minds and libraries still exist!

Do something further: impose on yourself, as a rule for your intelligence, to associate only with geniuses. How many geniuses there are who dominate the human horizon! You will never spend time with them all. So why waste time? From the religious point of view, as from the philosophical and scientific point of view, you must live with the highest minds. And do not tell me that you are too young to attend such a great school. If you want my opinion, nobody is as well understood as a genius. A genius who wants to be hidden would no longer be a genius. And what riches, light and enjoyment are found in their company! So, it is understood that in matters of religion, as in all things, you will always turn to the great masters, putting aside mediocrity. Remember the thought of St Augustine: "Everything that is done for the Kingdom of Heaven must be great, because nothing enters Heaven that is not great."

VII MEDITATION

Practices concerning the mind are necessary because the mind holds first place among the human faculties. But among the exercises of the mind there are two which I want to draw your attention to more vividly, and they are meditation and the examination of conscience. "Meditation is for religious!" you will tell me. Yes, it is certainly good for religious; but it might also be the best thing for you. And you will hardly become a sincere Christian until you are used to serious reflection, which is called meditation. Perhaps your idea of it is much more complicated than the reality.

But, tell me, do you know what it means to reflect; to reflect on something that you have read, on a thought that you find in your memory, on a teaching that you have listened to; to reflect on a duty to fulfil, on a job to be done, on a means to employ; that is, to carefully consider an issue that interests you, because it concerns your practical life and requires a decision? Who, then, does not (or does not know how to) reflect? A serious man is specifically called a thoughtful man. I am sure that you, who want to be a serious man, have already acquired habits of reflection, and reflect a great deal, perhaps because you are too restless about your present and your future. You know, therefore, how to reflect. Furthermore, you know what it means to pray. To pray is to stay with God, both in your interior sentiments and your external words. Since you want to be a Christian, you have already formed serious prayer habits; for you know that he who does not pray cannot be a Christian.

Since you know what it means to reflect and what it means to pray, you will learn how to meditate easily enough; because meditation is nothing other than the union of prayer with reflection. In whatever form you do it, and whatever method you choose to help you, you meditate when you reflect by praying, or pray by reflecting. And this is precisely what I want to suggest to you. In this union of prayer with reflection, which is meditation, you will find three considerable advantages:

1. Your prayers will become more serious, deeper, more alive. You will become accustomed to not mechanically re-

citing formulas, without tasting their meaning. You cannot imagine what depth of meaning is contained in the prayers of the Church. The *Pater*, for example, which you recite so often, is an infinite world. In the *Ave Maria*, in acts of faith, hope, charity and contrition, all of the words contain treasures. Is it not a shame to recite such beautiful things lightly? The mechanical recitation of vocal prayers is one sign of a superficial Christian, and leads man to lie to himself perpetually. The reality of the sentiments of his heart does not correspond to the words he utters. Such a lying practice, in one of the most sacred acts of life, is truly painful.

2. You will find another benefit in meditation: that of sanctifying and vivifying your activities. Your work is too natural; in the practical course of your daily life, God does not occupy the place that is due to Him. You distress yourself in a totally human movement, without letting God enter into the reflections and concerns that life imposes on you. Meditation, by getting you used to combining prayer with reflection, brings the supernatural element into the framework of your practical life.

3. And then there is a third advantage, which is the unity of your life. You are, at present, too much split in two. When you are at prayer, your mind is not altogether there; it tarries in external business and concerns. When you apply yourself to your work, God is not altogether there. Your prayer is not human enough and your work is not Christian enough. Your prayer is not human enough, because it is either too distracted or too abstract. In happy moments, it is too much made up of dreams and imagination, which you are tempted to consider as devotion; in the usual course of things,

it gets drawn into distractions. Your work is not Christian enough, because it is too natural and too earthly; you are not the same in church and at work. You are like a snake cut in two; the body moves in one direction, while the tail twists toward the other.

I would like to join these two sections of your life. I would like you to be one, the same everywhere, a Christian everywhere — at work as in prayer, in your life outside just as in church — putting God in first place everywhere, and then coming to love Him alone. The Christian is a man who is all of a piece, whose whole life is inspired by a single principle: that he is a man! The habit of meditation that I am recommending will lead you to become exactly this. When you know how to unite reflection with prayer, you will become a man, because, wherever you reflect, you will be led to pray, and wherever you pray, you will be led to reflect. Do you see how, when the serious and the supernatural join hands and embrace your whole life, then you become a Christian? Now I think you understand why and how I recommend meditation.

Do not ask me how to arrive there. There are so many methods that it would be very clumsy of me to try to choose one for you. Besides, I do not know you — you may not need any method; it may be that you need a very simple method; perhaps you are one of those who cannot take a step without the support of a complicated mechanism — that is for your director to decide. As is my wont, I am trying to highlight the first principles, leaving it to your good will to put them into practice.

Finally, you must understand that the meditation which I recommend to you does not consist entirely in a short exercise that you perform every morning by picking up a book on which you reflect before God. The half or quarter of an hour of reflection, which is commonly called "formal meditation", must only be the preparation of your real meditation, that is to say, of your meditative state. Insofar as you understand me, you must strive to become a reflective and praying man who routinely combines reflection with prayer throughout the day. And you must come to do so in a movement of simple, easy, practical life, equally devoid of naturalism and sentimentality, equally far from exaggeration and dissipation.

VIII   THE EXAMINATION OF CONSCIENCE

This, above all else, is a vital matter, for here lies the centre of the mechanism of the Christian life. You will soon understand why. You have a destination: God. You have a journey: conformity to the divine will. You have the means for the journey towards this destination: exercises of piety. Destination, journey, means — all of this must sustain itself, bind itself together and form one single thing. The destination requires the journey; the journey requires the means; the means must ensure the journey, which is the way to reach the destination. Is this not how you understand the Christian life?

What is it that connects the path to the destination and the means to the journey? Something is needed to ensure that your journey goes straight to the destination, and that your means efficiently favour your journey. You need to be aware of the destination, the journey and the means in order to correlate the means to the journey, and the journey to the destination, not in an isolated way, but in one and the same simultaneous view. Do not read this too quickly, please, because I want you to understand it properly — this more than thing else, for this is the crux of your life. I want your life to be one, and this is where you will find the practical means of truly making it one. If you do not try to get a clear and distinct idea of what I am telling you here, you will miss the best of this little work, because you will not see its chain of argument and you will be unable to implement it.

It is necessary, then, to see whether you really serve God, Who is the destination, and whether you serve Him first and alone; whether you live in conformity to God's will in acceptance and in action, which is the journey; and lastly, whether you employ useful exercises, which are the means. And you have to see these three things with a single look. How shall you see them? With an examination of conscience, which must pay attention to these three things. Are you heading to the destination? Are you on the right journey? Do you use effective means? If the examination does not look at these three things at the same time, it is insufficient and will not achieve its purpose.

You know that the questions asked in any examination are most important. In an examination of conscience, your entire life must be excavated to its very heart. One cannot be satisfied with a superficial glance, but must plumb the depths and reality of things. — "You are telling me that an

examination of conscience is a singularly difficult thing!"
— First of all, we agree that there cannot be a serious and
effective examination in any other way; so let us see whether
doing it in this way is in fact a difficult practice.

IX THE TRAIN DRIVER

The soul is one, but its internal dispositions are very varied.
Some are good, others bad. You have virtuous inclinations
and habits — such as self-sacrifice, humility, charity, sobriety
— but you also have perverse tendencies — such as pride
and sensuality, which are the two greatest. You act under the
influence of these inclinations and tendencies. Those that
are good make you go towards God; those that are bad make
you go towards yourself. In fact, you have understood that
there are only two directions in life: either the quest for God
or the quest for oneself. Consequently, the problem is very
simple: it can be summed up in whether you are engaged
in a quest for God or for yourself?

"But it does not seem completely simple to me. There are
so many tendencies in me, so many inclinations, so many
sentiments! How can I get to know them all? If I do not know
them all, I will never be sure that I am not deceiving myself."

Listen to me. There are several coaches in a train; each
coach has several wheels. How many wheels make the train
go! And they must all move, and must be pulled all together
in the same movement and kept in the same direction. The
driver in charge of regulating the journey of the train knows
this very well. However, do you think he thinks about the

number of wheels? It is the last thing he thinks about. Do you think he has to start each wheel rolling, one after the other? That would take him some time; and would be some journey! His job, however, is much simpler. He has, by his hand, a lever which controls the steam. When he wants to start the train, to make it move forward or backward, to accelerate or to decelerate, he places his hand on the lever, pulls lightly, and that is all! All the wheels move, and the whole train obeys the pull of a lever. You see what a great movement is started and directed by a single small action.

The same thing happens in your soul. However numerous its dispositions, however many its movements, it takes the slightest act to start each one in the right direction. It is no longer a question of taking every element, one by one; just as, for the driver, it is no longer a question of taking the wheels of his train one by one. — "But how is this possible?" you ask me. — Easily: it happens with the same simplicity with which the driver acts. — "Very well," you tell me, "but the simplicity of the driver's manoeuvre still supposes that the train is put together and that everything is in order. And the work of putting a train together is not just a matter of a simple hand gesture." — Yes, but, as far as your soul is concerned, rest assured: it is God Himself Who puts together the train. He has joined together your body and soul, your faculties, your dispositions and your attitudes. He has prepared the path of His will, on which you must walk. He kindles and maintains the fire of sanctifying grace, and the steam of actual grace.

No doubt you will need to take out and service each piece of the mechanism from time to time. This is what you must do in ordinary confessions, but, above all, in the annual practice, which must be the renewal of all the component parts of your soul. Such overhaul and repair work is of capital importance, but it is not what I want to teach you now. What I want to tell you here concerns only the journey of the train and the way to direct it. So, what do you have to do to ensure a good journey through life? Simply that which the driver has to do; that is, to carefully keep an eye out and to pull the lever which controls the steam accordingly. This is what is done in the examination of conscience. But here I must give the word for a moment to the author whose book has inspired the best reflections that I have presented to you so far. I dare to recommend that you read his work on those days when you decide to reflect seriously. He will profitably complete what I have been able to sketch only too imperfectly here.[11]

X THE INTERIOR GLANCE

How should the examination of conscience be done? With a glance. A glance where? To the centre of the heart. To see what? One thing only: the dominant disposition. And what is this dominant disposition? It is the feeling that moves the heart. In fact, I do nothing without my heart being pushed to do it by some thought or feeling which determines it. When

[11.] Dom Pollien is referring to his own work, *La vita interiore semplificata e ricondotta al suo fondamento*, first published in English as *The Interior Life Simplified and Reduced to Its Fundamental Principle*, edited by Very Rev Fr Joseph Tissot, M.S.F.S., translated by W.H. Mitchell, M.A., Burns Oates & Washbourne Ltd., London, 1912.

I ask someone, "Why are you doing this?" he replies, "For this reason." This reason is the thought that makes him act; and the thought is the dominant disposition of the heart at that moment.

It is this disposition, this thought, this feeling that the examination must attain. Why? Because this is what moves my heart and determines my conduct. When I hit on it, I know where I am and where I am going. If I am going straight (that is, to God) then everything is in order, and I have only to continue on my way. If I am going sideways (that is, towards my own satisfaction) I need to straighten out my intention.

"But is it easy to grasp this sentiment, this dominant disposition?" — Very easy: it only takes a glance. Where is my heart? I look and see very clearly whether it is going straight or not, and why it is going straight or not. When the eye is open, this jumps right out. — "Is this the whole examination?" — Yes, this is the whole of it; or at least what is essential. If this is not done, there can be no serious examination; when it is done, the examination is guaranteed.

"But what about other thoughts? Other feelings? And other actions?" — Thoughts and feelings that do not dominate are not dangerous. They are of no serious importance, except when they come to dominate, to direct the heart. But when they get to that point, they are in turn hit by the glance of the examination. When, subsequently, I grasp the good and bad feelings that make my heart move, then how deeply do I know my soul! I know all the mechanisms of the train; and, knowing that, it is easy to drive it. I have said "the good and bad feelings", because you must see the good as well as the bad, in order to know the state of the heart.

As for actions, knowledge of their number is not important except when it comes to mortal sins which must be confessed exactly; knowledge of other actions does not matter, except to help the knowledge of the dominant disposition which they make known.

"The examination of conscience, then, is very easy. It is the easiest thing of all, a glance. I can do it in an instant, as often as I want. But what about contrition? and amendment?" When you know how to do it, the glance contains all of this. I see, I repent, I rectify.[12]

XI THE SIMPLICITY OF THE GLANCE

To better understand the simplicity of this spiritual operation, which is needed to ensure a good course for your life, remember that your purpose is essentially one: to glorify God; that your journey is essentially one: to follow the will of God; that the multiple dispositions and movements of your soul must be dominated by grace, and that the main formative disposition of your piety is docility to God. What, therefore, must the glance assure you of? Of the existence of this dominant disposition in you, which commands everything.

Are you docile to God? In conclusion, this is what you must find out. If you are not, then you are not walking straight; if you are, you necessarily walk straight, and

[12] *Ibid.*, Part III, Book II, Chapter 9.

everything is fine. In fact, this is the real lever that controls the steam. When you are flexible and docile, your soul is open to the steam of grace, which rushes into the mechanism of your faculties and pulls them with all their movements in the direction of God's glory. If you are reluctant, the lever is closed, grace is blocked at the entrance, and the evil movement that keeps your soul closed to God carries you off in the wrong direction.

The glance has the sole purpose of verifying whether your soul is open or closed; of keeping it open when it is open and, if not, of opening it. Is it difficult, therefore? And what does it cost? Nothing, except sincerity. Are you resolved to be a Christian — not by halves, but seriously, thoroughly — a Christian without cowardice and without falsehood; yes or no? Everything lies there.

If you feel the need for God in your heart then I have nothing further to add: you have understood me. Go ahead resolutely, I am sure you will make progress and have a good journey. — "But is a glance enough to assure us of the existence of this main disposition, which is docility?" — Yes, and you will immediately understand why. When you are docile, grace enters in. Upon entering, it gives you light. This light is God's. And on what is it cast? On God, on you and on creatures: on God Who is your destination, in order to know Him as you must; on you, who are on the journey, in order to identify the defects that remain in you, the virtues that you lack, the results obtained, the dispositions to be changed, the needs to be satisfied and the resolutions to be taken; finally, on creatures, which are your means, to see which must be eliminated, and which must be used and how to use them.

With the help of this light, what do you see of God, of yourself and of creatures? As I have already said in the chapter on actual grace, you see exactly the points which are there to be seen, according to the current needs of your journey. So everything is well lit: the destiny, the journey and the means. And it is grace which brings all things to light. If you do not see them in the light of grace, you will never see anything; or you will see everything backwards. It is the glance that ensures that this light enters in. In this way, to know everything that you need to know, grace is needed; to introduce grace, docility is needed; to maintain docility, a glance is needed; for this glance, sincerity is needed: sincerity — that is, good will.

Do you understand, then, the fundamental operation of your journey in the Christian life? Do you understand its simplicity? Do you see how, in the final analysis, only one provision is required to fulfil all that the message of the Incarnation contains? This is the plan of God and your agenda: "Glory to God in the highest; and on earth peace to men of good will" (Lk 2:14). Good will. This is the only thing asked by God and sung by the angels.

I do not doubt that you have good will. No, there can be no question of falsehood and cowardice between us. Let me point out to you the only obstacle, which clashes with the good will of beginners and of ignorant people. They want, as is said, to "nit-pick"; and when that is not possible, they wander to and fro without profit. At first you will be tempted to find a glance too simple, and you will complicate it, believing that more needs to be done. Instead of submitting, through the intimate glance, practically and effectively to the action of God, you will upset everything, in order to see more and to do better. This means you will be led to rely still more on your own action rather than on God's. Have faith in the Saviour Who tells you "he that followeth me, walketh not in darkness, but shall have the light of life" (John 8:12). Yes, follow Him through the interior glance; keep your eye fixed on it, and you will see opportunities for virtue present themselves, resolutions imposed, vices shaken, transformations taking place, and your life developing. You will feel yourself become a Christian by the grace of God.

XII ON THE PATH TO HEAVEN

Now do you see clearly how to become a thoroughbred Christian. You are a Christian and on the path of life. I see you as a train driver who is given a beautiful and well-put-together train: cars, coaches, provisions, workers, everything is ready. The fires are lit, the steam is up: why is the train not moving? Pull the lever — and off it goes. This is you, this is your life. God Himself put together the train. He united the faculties of your soul and body: this is the train. He has prepared an infinity of provisions for you: all creatures. He lit the fire of grace; the way of His will is completely open. What do you need to do in order to start moving? One glance and a pull of the lever — and behold — grace transports you on the path of the will of God: in the direction of God's glory.

And to keep on this journey, you have no other job to perform than the driver's. Look at him in the act of glancing over the train, regulating its journey, maintaining the coal and water; he keeps his eye on the job. Keep your eye too on what you need to do. Watch over the movement of your soul; look at where you are, ensure docility. In the light of grace, take up those exercises of piety that are necessary for you, to maintain the fire of love and the steam of grace. And so, keep yourself in the direction of duty and submission to God, for His glory.

Can you really complain that this is difficult? Truly, what more could God do to facilitate holiness, except put you in the earthly paradise again, like Adam? Those who complain about God are as cowardly as they are ignorant! If you have understood what I have told you here, you are no longer ignorant. So, you will never be a coward: it would be too shameful for you. We are dealing with such a great thing, and it costs so little! And if nature sometimes finds the way hard, the fire of grace carries one to the peaks, if only one knows how to maintain it.

So, on the way to Heaven, you have everything you need! With you on the train are your patron saints, your good angel, Mary your Mother, Jesus Christ and God Himself. They accompany you, they protect you, they help you. Be worthy of their company, count on them to make up for your shortcomings, and — glory to God — you will progress. On the way to Heaven! The path is long: you must not waste time, strength or resources. You are only at the beginning of the journey; that is a good reason not to waste any of what you have. Show me now that you have faith, that you know what God is, what you are, what creatures are, what the way is, what Heaven is. On the way to Heaven!

XIII FINAL REFLECTIONS

A hundred times perhaps, while reading this book, you have felt your heart assaulted by this thought: "But this is exaggerated and impossible!" From the very first steps, if you remember well, I warned you about the inflexible rigour of the principles you were about to meet. Frequently along the way, I kept your spirit and heart roused. And now, at the end, I still feel the need to warn you against the arguments of cowards. The spirit of cowardice, inspired by the selfish instinct of enjoyment, oh how skilfully and how deeply it insinuates itself into our poor nature! Pleasure incessantly wants to pull us down and make us fall asleep at a rest stop.

And I long to lift you up. I wish (and how much I wish this) that you were a perfect Christian, complete, and "failing in nothing" (Jm 1:4). "For God is my witness, how I long after you all in the bowels of Jesus Christ. And this I pray, that your charity may more and more abound in knowledge, and in all understanding: that you may approve the better things, that you may be sincere and without offence unto the day of Christ, filled with the fruit of justice, through Jesus Christ, unto the glory and praise of God" (Phil 1:8-11).

I beseech you to climb and expand. In order to climb, be a man of principles. Only principles make men — and things — nothing is done without principles. Just try to make a chemical compound without respecting the laws and principles that govern it. When you do mathematical calculations, do you say: two and two are roughly four? Are the three angles of a triangle sometimes equal to two right angles? These things make you smile. Do you think principles are more necessary for a calculation, or to make a chemical compound, than to make a man? Are the fundamental principles of religion lesser principles than those of chemistry or mathematics? No. Without principles, nothing is done; neither in chemistry, nor in mathematics, nor in religion; nothing but ridiculous attempts and uncertain results. So, be a man of principles, and take up the laws of Christianity in their iron integrity, determined to follow them to the end. Do not try to adapt them to your whims; principles do not lend themselves to any adaptation: either they are, or they are not.

When it comes to the means, you can and must adapt. You have seen that the practice of the Christian life has to adapt to all situations, bend to everything and make use of everything. Firmness in principles, gentleness in means: this is the seal of truth. If you have the misfortune of breaking principles, it will always be to the benefit of your whims. And then you are like a ship without a compass, like a train without a track, like a leaf at the mercy of the wind. You know that whims are essentially changeable: those of today are not those of yesterday, nor those of tomorrow; such that your life, bending in the wind of your whims, makes you a weathervane. Alas, there are more weathervanes in houses than there are on roofs! What a sad comedy is a poor human life, tossed about from pleasure to pleasure, from trivial matter to trivial matter, from nothingness to nothingness! When men no longer live by principles, they are no longer men. You do not like the inflexibility of principles? Then do as Diogenes did: take a lantern and go in search of men. They say that it is men who are lacking; but I do not think so: it is principles which are lacking.[13] It is Fr Aubry, a thinker and a distinguished figure, who speaks thus. Yes, principles are lacking. And because they are lacking, men are no longer formed — Christians are no longer formed.

By taking up the pursuit of one's pleasure as if it were law, everyone diminishes and isolates himself within himself, because the whims, needs and tastes of one man are not those of another. Thus, each man has a law and an individual path, and so, in practice, we end up with divided ideas, competing interests, and chaos. There is no longer a common basis, no longer a possible understanding, no more union in anything, no more agreement in anything. It is confusion, it is weakness, it is ruin. That is where we are, and God knows where we are going. And it is the logical result of a life of attempts and uncertainties.

You who wish to be a man — and, above all, a Christian — leave behind, once and for all, the degraded world's ways of seeing and doing; resolutely shake off this life of

[13.] Fr Jean-Baptiste Aubry, *Essai sur la Méthode des Etudes ecclésiastiques en France, (Essay on the Methods of Ecclesiastical Studies in France)*, Part I, p. 265, Desclée de Brouwer, Lille, 1890.

selfish sentimentality, cowardly vanity and self-interested falsehood. Get off the muddy road. You will see that, if there is an immense work to do (and to redo) in our society, this means that it is possible to do it (and to redo it) in an immense way. What a beautiful course, open to men who know how to have a Christian mind and heart!

Here, I have shown you the principles which make Christian minds and hearts. Take them, unfold them, make them live in you. Go to this destination, make this journey, employ these means; and I assure you that you will be a Christian. You will be a Christian, and you will also work to make Christians. You will open the ways of life to others; by your activity, you will attract other souls, who also need to live. And you will all progress together, and Christian society will be rebuilt.

XIV BE A CHRISTIAN!

Now it is time to explain this expression to you, which is the substance of this book. I wanted to reserve this explanation for the end, because this title is the summary of everything I have tried to teach you.

"Be a Christian!" To be a Christian means to be formed in (and transformed into) the image of Christ. And who is Christ? If you want to have some understanding of the mystery of Christ, it is necessary to consider four things: 1) His divinity; 2) His humanity; 3) the union of these two natures in Him; 4) the suppression of the human person.

1) His divinity: He is God, perfect God. He is the Son of God, the second of the Divine Persons. He is God from

eternity and for all eternity. God does not change (cf. Malachi 3:6).

2) His humanity: He is man, perfect man. He has a human nature — the whole of human nature; he has human faculties and qualities — all human faculties and perfections. Like you, He has a soul, a body, a mind, a will and senses. And He is more perfect than you in everything.

3) The union of these two natures in Him: the divine nature and human nature are united in Him; united, but not mixed, not confused; united, but without alteration, nor lessening, nor any change in the nature of God or in the nature of man. He is at the same time perfect God and perfect man. The divinity retains His infinite perfection, since He cannot change. Humanity retains all its integrity, since it is through the perfection of man that union becomes possible between God and man.

4) The suppression of the human person: in Jesus Christ, the Second Person of the Holy Trinity is hypostatically united to human nature. What does this mean? It means that the human person is absorbed into and is the same as the Divine Person; and that Our Lord's human nature — which possesses all the perfection of activity and operation to which a human being is susceptible — can in no way determine itself, nor move by itself. In the same way that the movements of your body are produced in you by your soul, so the determining impulse in and directing dominion over the Saviour's human actions come from the Divine Person. Just as the body is only capable of any activity when animated by the soul, so the human nature in Jesus Christ is only capable of being moved by the Divine Person.

Here is Christ, and here is the Christian. Christ continually exhorts you to be a Christian; the Christian, in order to bear the image of Christ, must have the four characteristics above, in the measure proper to him. We talk unceasingly about Christian life, piety, education, formation, society, Christian institutions, etc. Do those who say this word "Christian" so often know what it means? Do you have a clear idea of what it means? Remember that you cannot and must not apply the label of "Christian" unless you find together the four characteristics, that make up Christ: 1) the perfect divine element; 2) the perfect human element; 3) the union of the divine and the human; 4) the annihilation of human independence before God.

Everything in Jesus Christ was perfect from the beginning. His life was a fullness that could have an exterior growth only in its human element. Your own life is a seed that must develop until you are a perfect man — "unto the measure of the age of the fulness of Christ" (Eph 4:13). Consequently, you must become a Christian — that is to say, you must work within yourself to perfect the divine, the human, their union and the submission of the human to the divine. The work and purpose of the Christian is the perfecting of these four characteristics. Here is a final word about each, in order to see how they are contained in the four parts of this book:

1) The divine element: the glory of God is the divine element of your life. You see with what insistence I have asked you to expand it in yourself. The whole of this book resounds with it.

2) The human element: the faculties of your soul and your body — of your mind, your heart and your senses — are the human element. Have I recommended often enough that you develop them? Have I begged you often enough not to drift along, occupied with trivial matters?

3) The union of the divine and the human: do you not remember how much I preached to you, in Part Two, the union with God alone and absolute detachment from everything that is not Him?

4) Submission of the human to the divine: in Part Three, what did I do but teach you to submit and conform your actions in everything to the will of God — to let yourself be led and directed by Him?

Did I show you the background of the work of a Christian? Now you do the work, and when you have magnified God's glory in you to the highest possible level; when you have magnified your powers, your union with God and your submission to His action, then you will be worthy of your divine model. You will be a perfect Christian.

What splendour is in the Christian soul! O Jesus, how little-known is the meaning of this word, which is talked about so much! If it were known, we would not have the audacity to call by the name of Christian those people and things which are unworthy of Thee — who resemble Thee so little and take so little care to resemble Thee — who, even if they did make an effort, have such little knowledge! To be a Christian, to wish to be one; what a great thing, and it is something so rare!

XV EXHORTATION

See, then, the great horizons open before your eyes, the great spaces before your heart and the great course of the Christian life before your feet. I wanted to reveal them to you without mitigation, to show you their beauty, to reveal their magnitude and extent to you. I believe that a great heart such as yours — a strong, frank and upright heart — needs such space to expand. I groan when I see the little things in which you are too often forced to drift. Oh, how much fresh air, good food and vigorous exercise are needed — for your soul more than for your body! This is what I have wished to give you.

Tell me, is what I have presented to you suitable to your constitution? Do you feel that this armour of the strong is made for your frame? Can I, in conclusion, address to you St Paul's invitation to the Ephesians? "Finally, brethren, be strengthened in the Lord, and in the might of his power. Put you on the armour of God, that you may be able to stand against the deceits of the devil. For our wrestling is not against flesh and blood; but against principalities and powers, against the rulers of the world of this darkness, against the spirits of wickedness in the high places. Therefore take unto you the armour of God, that you may be able to resist in the evil day, and to stand in all things perfect. Stand therefore, having your loins girt about with truth, and having on the breastplate of justice, and your feet shod with the preparation of the Gospel of peace: in all things taking the shield of faith, wherewith you may be able to extinguish all the fiery darts of the most wicked one. And take unto you the helmet of salvation, and the sword of the Spirit which is the word of God" (Eph 6:10-18). Such is the armour of the soldier of God: well tempered and giving the certainty of splendid victories.

Do you want to be a soldier of God? Do you feel the passion of a great heroism quivering in your veins? Do the great battles of faith not call victoriously upon your generosity? Yes, I am sure of it, you are moved by the warlike ardour which makes great Christians. Never will you passively watch the assaults multiplying on all sides against that which is most precious in the world — that which is dearest in your life — that which you would be happy to give your blood for: your faith, your religion, your God.

Yes, it takes men to defend this great cause; it is so weakly and so deplorably defended by so many. God and the Church ask for defenders, but true defenders; those who will never take a step back; those who know how to be faithful until death; those who are trained in all the severities of discipline, to be ready for all the heroic struggle. The severities of discipline I have mapped out for you in this book. Take them up, let none of them frighten you, then you will not be afraid of any struggle; not only that, but you will not miss any triumph. The powerlessness, division and weakening of the good comes from the fact that they have loosened the armour of the strong and the discipline of heroes; and this is what makes up the strength of bad men. Take back the armour, regain your discipline, and you will be strong — strong like the heroes of the great ages of faith — and then you must fight magnificent battles and gain splendid victories.

Yes, certainly there is a lot to do in the world today; and whatever people say, life opens up beautifully to the impulses of those who have ideas in their heads, love in their hearts and blood in their veins. Do you have any of this? Yes, you have it, you have the Christian idea in your head, Christian love in your heart, Christian blood in your veins. You have this idea, this love and this Christian blood. I set out to excite them in you. I wanted to arouse the enthusiasm of the Christian idea in your head, foment outpourings of Christian love in your heart, and stimulate the generosity of Christian blood in your veins.

Go now and say: "Glory to God! There are noble things to do, and I will do them! There is a power in the world, which triumphs over the world and everything in it, and this power is the Christian faith. I have this faith and I am very happy now to be able to answer the question with all truth, with which this book begins: 'Do you believe in God?' I found it so strange then! Now I understand it better; and understanding it better, I say with all the sincerity of my soul: I believe in God, I will love God, I will serve God, I will be a Christian!"